WARRIOR IN TRAINING

Sabrina Louise Miller

Page 26, 44, 118, 157, 183 - Oswald Chambers, July 2nd, My Utmost For His Highest

Page 72 - Table of Grace, Phillips, Craig and Dean

New King James Version (NKJV). Scripture quotations marked NKJV are taken from *The New King James Version*. Copyright 1979, 1980, 1982, Thomas Nelson, Inc.

The Living Bible (TLB). Verses marked TLB are taken from *The Living Bible* 1971. Used by permission of Tyndale House Publishers, Inc., Wheaton, Illinois 60189. All rights reserved.

New Living Translation (NLT). Scripture quotations marked NLT are taken from *Holy Bible, New Living Translation*, copyright 1996. Used by permission of Tyndale House Publishers, Inc., Wheaton, Illinois 60189. All rights reserved.

Warrior in Training
ISBN: 0-88144-373-5
Copyright © 2009 by Sabrina Miller

Published by
Thorncrown Publishing
A Division of Yorkshire Publishing Group
9731 East 54th Street
Tulsa, Oklahoma 74146
www.yorkshirepublishing.com

- *Series I* -

The Making of A Warrior

Table of Contents

The Making of A Warrior

So you want to be a warrior...
Stop and count the cost!
Many called, few chosen,
Of those few...none lost.

The warrior life is lonely...
Until His presence you receive!
Wait in expectation,
He will come if you believe.

Only warriors stand until the end...
Following each and every command!
Their voices declaring victory,
Throughout this... our promised land.

He is calling you, O warrior...
The journey may seem far away!
But His presence will be your strength,
As you live from day to day.

Introduction

Warrior In Training

Warrior In Training. It sounds awfully heroic, but I can assure you that becoming a warrior for Christ is a life-long experience, an experience that will require you to lay your life down daily. I, personally, would never have known these principles had the Lord not brought these truths to me at my church, Immanuel Baptist Church, Skiatook, OK. Under the prophet, Dr. Jim D. Standridge and many other wonderful teachers, the Lord has taught me to not only become a *Warrior In Training* but to impart these truths to others. You will find many of their life-teachings in this manual. I have made them mine and lived them out. This manual is a compilation of our hearts towards the warrior concept. It matters not whether you are male or female, I believe the Lord has effectively allowed this *Warrior In Training* manual to be genderless.

As you study these truths, which originated with the Heavenly Father, they will become yours. I pray that you will find yourself changed at the end of the journey and can say with me, *"I have found the Lord to be faithful."*

Each day, work through one "day" in your manual. If you are asked a question, write down your answer. If you are given an assignment, do it. Your level of commitment to do the work will determine the level of change in your life at the end of the year. As you work through your book, should you miss a day, do your best to get caught up. Each day has a short devotion. Next, you will read one chapter of Proverbs. There are thirty-one chapters in Proverbs, so you will be reading the chapter that corresponds with that particular day of the month. (For example, if it is the third day of the month, read the third Proverb.) There is also a Proverb Journal at the beginning of each week. You will write down at least one idea you specifically received from reading that particular chapter. After twelve months of consistently reading Proverbs, you will have your very own Proverbs commentary.

You have two verses to memorize each week. At the beginning of each month, you will find a place to mark that you have done your reading and praying for each day. The goal is to build consistency in your life.

Reading the Word of God daily is going to change your life. I can promise you that if you will give your heart to the promises of God, you will have the exciting opportunity of watching your life change. Remember, the purpose of a study such as this is that you might come to know Him in a very personal way. May the Lord richly bless your efforts.

Sabrina Louise Miller

Foreword

So, you want to be a *Warrior in Training,* or do you? You may not fully recognize what it will cost to be called a *Warrior In Training.* In order to help you understand more about what you plan to embrace with your entire life, let me explain where this concept came from. The *Warrior In Training* concept was originally formed in 1993 by my mother, the author of this manual, Sabrina Miller. She formed the ministry out of a realization of how desperately she needed the Lord to touch her life. She understood how important a daily walk with the Lord was and knew the impact it could have on a group of young people who were willing to accept this challenge from God. She found this group at Immanuel Baptist Church, Skiatook, OK. These young people began to live through a great time of ministry and revival. The Lord began to use them to shake, not only their small town, but in many aspects, the nation. They ministered to one another, their community and their school. It became known as "The Great Adventure" in 1994. Sabrina and her husband, Stan, loaded up some forty young people along with their leadership team and embarked on a one-week tour of the southeastern U.S. They traveled through three states and performed ten services. They saw the Lord move in miraculous ways. I was seven at the time and traveled with the team on this great trip. I watched as these young people were transformed. I can personally speak of the mighty move of God and the shaking and awakening it had on each life it touched.

This life-altering manual is being placed in your grasp. Simply put words, yet divinely imparted with the grace and power of our Lord Jesus Christ, breaking down strongholds and birthing a deep passion unlike any you've experienced. If you will only give yourself to this book, allow the Lord to speak into you through it and discipline yourself to it, the Lord will show you His face, His might and His power. However, this is no idle commitment. To see your life changed, you will have to give yourself to it daily. Webster defines a warrior as a *"person engaged in some struggle or conflict."* We (believers) fight a very real enemy and this training manual will teach you the keys to victory and an overcoming lifestyle. I ask three things of you as you begin to pursue the lifestyle of a warrior:

1. That you would discipline yourself daily to dig into the Word and teachings. You will get out what you put in so put in all of yourself that you may receive all the Lord has for you.

2. That you not only experience this manual, but passionately give your heart to the Lord and open your mind to His unction.

3. That you be willing to undergo the changes this book will require. Often, following the Lord's will for your life is a painful experience. When He places you on the potter's wheel and smashes you from what you felt was a finished work into a pile of lumpy clay, you will desire to quit. However, if you push on, I can attest from experience that He is faithful to His workmanship and will do that which is promised in His Word.

I encourage you to embrace this challenge. Allow God to do in you what He's done in so many others through this teaching. May the Lord bless and keep you and show you His goodness and mercy.

Skylar Miller

Will You Follow Me

Will you follow me in discipleship?
He speaks the words straight to your heart.
It will cost you everything to answer the question.
Count the cost before you start.

Following Me you will find your life.
But you must first be willing to give it up.
I only ask you to walk the path I have walked.
Are you willing to drink from death's cup?

Oh, Jesus, I long to follow you.
Crucify my resistance and my plans.
I place my life in Your sovereign keeping,
As I choose to submit to Your Kingdom demands.

Make me a disciple, Lord.
My Kingdom destiny fulfill.
Let the crucifixion process work in my life,
Keep my passion alive and real.

THE MAKING OF
A WARRIOR

MONTH ONE

The Beginning of Discipleship
Month One - Week One

Week One Checklist

To keep track of how consistent you are becoming in your walk as a disciple, check off your work on this chart as you go. You will either be encouraged as you see your progress or challenged as you see your inconsistency. I am praying that you will be the *"workman that needeth not be ashamed."*

	Bible Study	Memory	Proverbs	Prayer
Sunday	_____	_____	_____	_____
Monday	_____	_____	_____	_____
Tuesday	_____	_____	_____	_____
Wednesday	_____	_____	_____	_____
Thursday	_____	_____	_____	_____
Friday	_____	_____	_____	_____
Saturday	_____	_____	_____	_____

Prayer Requests

_____

_____

_____

_____

_____

_____

Memory Verses
Month One - Week One

Mark 8:34
*"Whosoever will come after me, let him deny himself,
and take up his cross and follow me."*

Mark 8:35
*"For whosoever will save his life shall lose it; but whosoever
shall lose his life for My sake and the gospel's, the same shall save it."*

PROVERBS JOURNAL

Proverbs Chapter _____ _____
_____

Proverbs Chapter _____ _____
_____

Proverbs Chapter _____ _____
_____

Proverbs Chapter _____ _____
_____

Proverbs Chapter _____ _____
_____

Proverbs Chapter _____ _____
_____

Proverbs Chapter _____ _____
_____

A DISCIPLE
One who follows his leader!

The Beginning of Discipleship
Month One - Week One

Day One

If you are a follower of Jesus Christ, then you are called to "discipleship." This particular study is especially written to assist you in learning how to do that. Oswald Chambers said, *"Faith never knows where it is being led but it knows and loves the one who is leading."* Becoming a disciple is an act of faith. Discipleship is not an option—it's a mandate. Jesus said we were to go and make disciples. (Matthew 28:19.) Before we can fulfill that call, we must first *become* a disciple. As a disciple, you must be willing to take personal responsibility for developing "excellence" in the basics of discipleship. If you are willing to do that, then this study in discipleship will change your life forever. ***Excellency is to go beyond the normal standard, to achieve more than is expected of an average person.***

Completing this course will cost you time and effort. However, the results of giving yourself to a consistent prayer life, Bible study and memorization will be of immeasurable value to you. As a disciple of Jesus, you are entitled to a river of abundance, but you must first get in the river to receive its refreshing. Are you ready to begin the exciting adventure of discipleship? This adventure will continue throughout your lifetime. Following or resisting—there are really only two options. Be encouraged as you begin, it's a process.

IF YOU WILL BE FAITHFUL TO START IT,
HE WILL BE FAITHFUL TO COMPLETE IT.

Let's begin the week by memorizing the following two memory verses:

Mark 8:34b   *"Whosoever will come after me, let him deny himself, and take up his cross and follow me."*

Mark 8:35   *"For whosoever will save his life shall lose it; but whosoever shall lose his life for My sake and the gospel's, the same shall save it."*

Remember, a disciple is *"one who follows his leader."*

Answer the following questions:

1. Has there ever been a time in your life when you realized you were a sinner?

2. Have you come to realize that you could never save yourself by your good works or good character?

3. Do you believe that Jesus Christ died on the cross for you, offering His life as a substitute for your sins?

4. Have you accepted Christ as your personal Savior and Lord? If so, when?

If you could answer *yes* to all four questions above, then you are ready to be a disciple of Jesus Christ. If you could not answer yes, then turn to the Plan Of Salvation at the end of this book and let me share with you how you might come to know Him.

To begin our Bible study, I want to introduce you to John, the evangelist. He wrote the fourth gospel. John's gospel tells more about Jesus than any other gospel. You'll love reading the book of John. With the Holy Spirit's help, he will paint pictures of the life of Christ. As you study, I encourage you to imagine yourself there with Christ in the story as one of the disciples, a follower. Allow the words John penned to change you and direct you to the purpose of your life.

Today, your reading assignment is John, Chapter 1. After you've read it, answer the following questions.

1. Who is the Word?

2. Do you see see the Word as Jesus?

3. Why was John sent from God?

4. As a believer of Jesus, what have you received from God according to this? (v.12)

5. What was made flesh and dwelt among us?

6. Who did John testify that he was?

7. Who confessed, "I am not the Christ"?

8. What were the names of the four disciples who chose to follow Christ in verses 37-51?

As you study the life of John, I want to encourage you to put yourself in his place. What would it be like to follow the Lord Jesus everyday? Do you imagine that John saw him as a mere man more than God's son? It's hard for us to imagine how he felt as he witnessed miracles being done nearly every day. John was very affected by Jesus. You can tell that by his writings. I love all the gospels but John's stories seem so alive to me. Ask the Lord to take you into these stories as you read. Expect to be changed as you give yourself to the Word of God.

Read the proverb of the day and write in your journal.

Day Two

Today, let's take a closer look at your memory verse.

Mark 8:34b   *"Whosoever will come after me, let him deny himself, and take up his cross, and follow me."*

As one who follows his leader, you must be willing to die to yourself. Many believers are very excited about following Jesus. They want the peace and the comfort that only He can bring, but when they begin to see the cost, they turn and follow Him no more. John 6:66 says, *"From that time many of His disciples went back and walked no more with Him."* What about you?

You will either follow the Lord or, in resisting Him, you will follow your own way. Some people mistake self-denial as death to self; a legalist lifestyle of do's and don'ts. Don't drink, don't smoke, don't gamble. Legalism will never produce a disciple. To deny yourself means that you are so in love with your Master that you are willing to serve Him by giving up all rights to yourself. Jesus is looking for the one who will surrender their heart and all of it's attitudes and motives. When you become a disciple of Jesus Christ, you surrender your rights. You give up your own life, your own way and take on the heart of Christ—"a heart that cannot be offended." Are you willing to die to yourself? Even if you are hesitant, you serve a God that will make you willing if He sees only a spark of desire. Stay in process and watch the Lord win your heart. I know because He was passionate and persistent in winning mine in spite of all my resisting and stubbornness to follow.

Today, before you do your daily reading, write out a prayer asking the Lord to teach you what it means, personally, in your life to *die to yourself*.

Dear Jesus,

_____

_____

_____

_____

_____

_____

_____

_____

Today, read John, Chapter 2 and answer the following questions.

1. What was Jesus' first miracle?

2. How did the disciples react to this miracle?

3. How did Jesus react to the money changers in the temple at Jerusalem?

4. Is the sanctuary a holy place to you?

5. Have you ever had Jesus perform a miracle in your life?

6. What was your reaction to that miracle?

Maybe, as you begin this study, you need a miracle. Maybe you find yourself in a problem that seems overwhelming and hopeless. Every time we have a problem, we have the opportunity for a miracle. That miracle, no matter how small, is a testimony of what happens when Jesus comes on the scene. Jesus desires that we follow Him, not for what He can do for us but for who He is. Will you follow Him?

A MIRACLE IS AN EARTHLY EVENT…
…WITH A HEAVENLY EXPLANATION

Read the proverb of the day and write in your journal.

Day Three

Fill in the blank spaces.

So far, we have learned that we are called to be a _____ of Jesus. In order to be a _____, we must be willing to die to _____. Today, let's look at our memory verse, Mark 8:35a, *"For whosoever will save his life shall lose it; but whosoever shall lose his life for My sake and the gospel's, the same shall save it."*

The world teaches us that we should hang on to everything we can and seek to gain all that we can. To be a disciple is to do exactly the opposite. Jesus wants us to give up our ideas of what our life should be and let Him make the choices. We need to let Him write the story.

JESUS ALWAYS GIVES THE BEST…
…TO THOSE WHO LEAVE THE CHOICE UP TO HIM

This does not mean that we sit idly by and do nothing. On the contrary, we live our lives expecting Him to lead and guide us. We learn how to follow Him by studying His Word.

Read John, Chapter 3 and answer the following questions:

1. List three things you learned from the story of Nicodemus in Chapter 3.

    a)

    b)

    c)

2. List two things "light" does in one's life.

    a)

    b)

3. What does verse 30 mean to you?

4. Rewrite verse 36 in your own words.

5. Who does God give the Holy Spirit to?

Maybe you haven't realized the Holy Spirit's work in your life. Oswald Chambers says, *"The Holy Spirit is the experimental name for Eternal Life working in human beings here and now. The Holy Spirit is the Deity in proceeding power who applies the Atonement to our experiences."* The Holy Spirit is the third part of the Godhead. He is the voice of God at work in your life. When you received Jesus as your Lord and Savior, you received the Holy Spirit. Many believers ignore the Spirit's voice. That would be like walking down a dark road, having a flashlight in your hand and never turning it on. You have God through the Holy Spirit to direct you, to give you instruction. Are you listening to Him?

The Holy Spirit will guide you as you seek to follow the Lord and His commands. He is the still, small voice of God at work in your life. Let's pray together and ask for His guidance. Please pray with me.

Dear Holy Spirit,

Thank You for Your presence in my life. Forgive me for not listening to You and obeying Your prompting. I pray that You would give me a new awareness of Your presence and purpose in my life. I pray that I would be sensitive to You as you operate in my life. I ask You to fill me and guide me daily as I follow Jesus. Give me a new awareness of Your presence. I welcome You, Holy Spirit, as my friend and my comforter. In Jesus name, Amen.

Read the proverb of the day and write in your journal.

Day Four

Start your study today by writing out your memory verses. (Remember, the only way you are going to be changed is by bringing God's Word into your life.) Don't skip the memorization work.

Mark 8:34b

_____

_____

_____

Mark 8:35

_____

_____

_____

You can't expect to just wake up one day and find yourself a disciple. Let's look at this. Who is the one person in your life that you would like to pattern your spiritual walk after? Well, that person has disciplined themselves to become who they are. Probably you have watched as they have changed to become who they are now. However, too many times, we just practice the "discipline" and miss the whole call of "discipleship." A true disciple follows out of love for his master. The Lord doesn't want to make you a clone of the one you are watching. He made you with unique qualities and talents but He does want you to learn from others so you can apply the truth to who you are.

I bet the biggest problem that you are having is finding enough time to do this study, right? I find that most people spend time on the things they enjoy and love; things such as sports, movies, video games and shopping. I realize it will cost you something to finish this course. There will be many days you won't want to read or pray. I promise you that although your memory work may seem meaningless to you, there will be great benefits. There will be many times in your journey that you will have to choose - choose to discipline yourself to study. Remember, you have an enemy. His name is Satan and he hates the life of God in you. Your memorization of the scriptures will be a weapon against him. Quote your scriptures out loud when you don't want to do your study. Those verses will be your weapon to destroy the enemy. Please, don't just study because you want to be disciplined. I pray that you will study because you love Jesus with all your heart and long to know Him more.

Read John, Chapter 4 today and answer the following questions:

1. Why was the Samaritan woman surprised to have Jesus ask her for a drink? (v. 9)

2. What did Jesus tell this woman the "living water" could do for her?

3. What did you learn about true worshippers in this chapter?

4. Is following and obeying Jesus as important to you as your daily food?

5. Where did Jesus perform the second miracle?

Place the following in the order of importance in your life (be honest). **Number of**
Note: 1=least important. 10=most important. **Importance**

1. Participating in sports; basketball, baseball, football, soccer, hockey, fishing, etc.   _____

2. Reading your Bible   _____

3. Eating   _____

4. Sleeping   _____

5. Shopping   _____

6. Attending church   _____

7. Work or school   _____

8. Praying   _____

9. Watching television, movies or playing video games   _____

10. Spending time with friends   _____

Are you satisfied with that order of importance? Is the Lord pleased?

Read the proverb of the day and write in your journal.

Day Five

Sometimes we get the idea that following Jesus should be easy. Believe me, making a disciple out of you will take nothing short of a miracle. There are places in your life where you are "crippled" and can't do what following Jesus requires. Trust me, I know. I was very crippled and damaged in many ways. It has taken a miracle of grace for the Lord to change me. That's how I know you can be changed. Let me ask you a question, "Will you be made whole?"

Read John, Chapter 5 and answer the following questions:

1. It may seem like a strange question but why do you think Jesus asked the lame man at the pool if he wanted to be made whole?

2. In verses 17-19, what is Jesus telling us?

3. How does that apply to our lives?

4. In verse 30, what "will" does Jesus see?

When I came to Jesus at the age of 27, someone gave me my first copy of *"My Utmost For His Highest"* by Oswald Chambers. I have read it every morning since.

Oswald Chambers (1874-1917) died a man totally committed to hearing God's Word and abiding in Him. He started where many of us have been. He thought the Bible was dry and boring. Soon, Chambers realized he couldn't force himself to be holy. He realized the strength and peace he was looking for was Christ himself, Christ's life in exchange for his sin. Once he happened upon this realization, he experienced great renewal; so much so that he described it as a "radiant, unspeakable emancipation." Emancipation means, *"being set free."* We call that the *"exchanged life."*

Only one of Chambers' works were written by the man himself. The remaining thirty plus books bearing his name were compiled by his wife, Bitty, from dictations she had taken while her husband lectured at Bible Training College, founded by Chambers in 1911.

I want to encourage you to purchase a copy of this devotional and make it a daily part of your study time.

Please read the following:

OSWALD CHAMBERS

"Will you continue to go with me?"

It is true that Jesus Christ is with us in our temptations, but are we going with Him in His temptations? Many of us cease to go with Jesus from the moment we have an experience of what He can do. Watch when God shifts your circumstances and see whether you are going with Jesus or siding with the world, the flesh and the devil. We wear His badge but are we going with Him? "From that time many of His disciples went back and walked no more with Him."

The temptations of Jesus continued throughout His earthly life, and they will continue throughout the life of the Son of God in us. Are we going with Jesus in the life we are living now?

We have the idea that we ought to shield ourselves from some of the things God brings around us. Never! God engineers circumstances and whatever they may be like we have to see that we face them while abiding continually with Him in His temptations. They are His temptations, not temptations to us, but temptations to the life of the Son of God in us. The honor of Jesus Christ is at stake in your bodily life. Are you remaining loyal to the Son of God in the things which beset His life in you?

Do you continue to go with Jesus? The way lies through Gethsemane, through the city gate, outside the camp; the way lies alone, and the way lies until there is no trace of a footstep left, only the voice, "Follow me."

*(Oswald Chambers, September 19th)

Read the proverb of the day and write in your journal.

Day Six

Friendship is such a wonderful thing. Everyone needs friends, but there are seasons in our life when Jesus wants us all to Himself. Do you consider Jesus to be your best friend?

Who are your two closest friends? What if they decided that following Jesus was simply too difficult? Would that make a difference in your commitment to follow? Remember, a disciple is a follower of Jesus Christ. Please don't be surprised if one day you find yourself following Him alone. The Lord plans these times to bring us closer to His side.

Read John, Chapter 6 and answer the following questions:

1. a) Why did the multitude follow Him?

   b) Why do you follow Him?

2. What need did the miracle in chapter 6 meet?

3. What is the bread of God?

4 What does Jesus say is the will of God in verses 39 and 40?

5. a) How can a man come to Jesus?

   b) Were you drawn? (This is a really important question.)

   c) Is there any other way?

6. a) In John 6:66, many of the disciples ceased to follow Him. What question does He ask of the twelve disciples in verse 67?

   b) May I ask you, will you also go away?

THOUGH NONE GO WITH ME

I've heard the call to follow.
I've left personal dreams and plans behind.
I'm trusting in daily surrender,
As each morning Your will I find.

There are many worldly distractions.
Each one with an enticing call.
I have separated my heart to Your keeping.
I'll follow Lord, though it costs me all.

I give You my friends, my time, my family,
I give You all my life could be.
Following You as a faithful disciple,
Though none go with me, Jesus, my Destiny!

Write out your memory verses below and explain them in your own words.

Mark 8:34b

_____
_____
_____
_____

Mark 8:35

_____
_____
_____
_____

Read the proverb of the day and write in your journal.

Day Seven

If I just met you and knew nothing of Jesus, share with me how accepting Him as Savior has changed your life.

_____

_____

_____

_____

_____

_____

_____

_____

_____

_____

_____

_____

_____

_____

_____

_____

_____

_____

_____

_____

_____

_____

_____

_____

_____

Read the proverb of the day and write in your journal.

The Beginning of Discipleship
Month One - Week Two

Week Two Checklist

To keep track of how consistent you are becoming in your walk as a disciple, check off your work on this chart as you go. You will either be encouraged as you see your progress or challenged as you see your inconsistency. I am praying that you will be the *"workman that needeth not be ashamed."*

	Bible Study	Memory	Proverbs	Prayer
Sunday	_____	_____	_____	_____
Monday	_____	_____	_____	_____
Tuesday	_____	_____	_____	_____
Wednesday	_____	_____	_____	_____
Thursday	_____	_____	_____	_____
Friday	_____	_____	_____	_____
Saturday	_____	_____	_____	_____

Prayer Requests

_____

_____

_____

_____

_____

_____

Memory Verses
Month One - Week Two

Luke 14:26
"If any man come to me and hate not his father, and mother, and wife and children, and brethren, and sisters, yea, and his own life also, he cannot be my disciple."

Matthew 16:24
"Then Jesus said unto his disciples, 'If any man will come after me, let him deny himself, and take up his cross, and follow me.'"

PROVERBS JOURNAL

Proverbs Chapter _____ _____

_____

Proverbs Chapter _____ _____

_____

Proverbs Chapter _____ _____

_____

Proverbs Chapter _____ _____

_____

Proverbs Chapter _____ _____

_____

Proverbs Chapter _____ _____

_____

Proverbs Chapter _____ _____

_____

A DISCIPLE
One who loves his master above all else!

The Beginning of Discipleship
Month One - Week Two

Day One

Begin by looking at your memory verses for this week.

Luke 14:26 — *"If any man come to me and hate not his father, and mother, and wife and children, and brethren, and sisters, yea, and his own life also, he cannot be my disciple."*

Matthew 16:24 — *"Then Jesus said unto his disciples, 'If any man will come after me, let him deny himself, and take up his cross, and follow me.'"*

The focus of these verses is the Father's desire for you to love Him above everyone and everything. So many people think that following Jesus requires wearing a long face and NEVER having fun. That is NOT TRUE. He longs to give you your heart's desire, but you must go through the discipleship process and allow Him to become first in all things. Don't place your confidence in your sincerity to follow Him. When the rich young ruler came to Jesus, he had a sincere desire to follow Him. When Jesus put His finger on what was stopping the rich young ruler from becoming a true disciple, he could go no further because his money was more important to him than a relationship with Christ. Is there anything in your life more important than the Lord Jesus? If there is, would you be willing to surrender that particular relationship issue to Jesus today? As a beautiful warrior woman once shared with me, *"Jesus can only fill empty hands."*

A DISCIPLE IS ONE WHO LOVES
HIS MASTER ABOVE ALL ELSE

Begin your memory work and write out a prayer. Ask the Lord to bless your week of study and open your eyes and heart to the call of discipleship, making it personal to you!

Dear Lord,

_____

_____

_____

_____

DISCIPLESHIP

Open my eyes, Lord, to Your plan,
Following You is my desire.
Teach me from Your word and let me see,
What discipleship will require.

I don't want to be an ordinary person.
May the world see a difference, I pray.
In order to fulfill my destiny, Lord,
May I be willing to die each day to my way.

The world offers many options to me.
From sports to popularity and fame.
But I have seen Your face and believe,
That happiness is found in pursuit of Your name.

You have called me from my wanderings.
Many dreams and plans for me You have shown.
I'll study Your Word and apply myself,
As I live to make Your message known.

DOCTRINE IS SOMETHING THAT IS BEING TAUGHT AS TRUTH

Read John, Chapter 7 and answer the following questions:

1. There is so much wrong teaching today. In verse 17, how does Jesus say we can know His doctrine?

2. What is Jesus teaching us in verse 24?

   How does that principle affect you personally?

3. In verse 37-39, Jesus speaks of "a river of living water." How does Jesus say we can receive this water?

4. The religious people didn't believe Jesus was a prophet. Why?

To be a disciple not only requires discipline from you, but it also has its rewards. He will pour out His Spirit on those who are willing to go all the way with Him.

The passage in John 7 is speaking of one of those rewards. As a disciple, you will encounter the enemy and all his tactics. *For to be in the presence of God is to be in the presence of the enemy.* But, you will not be without His protection and His presence. He will bring peace and comfort to you as you follow Him. Think of the last time you were being attacked by the enemy, whether it was one of Satan's cohorts or a fellow soldier.

List below what you learned about the "character of God" from what He allowed you to go through.

_____

_____

_____

_____

_____

_____

_____

_____

A lot of people quit following Jesus because they don't want to endure the suffering that goes with discipleship. Suffering is designed to purify us. As we become desperate through suffering, we find Jesus in the manner John is speaking of. He becomes "life" to us. A river that flows through us, filling us with hope and peace. Suffering awakens us to how big God really is as we learn to cry out to Him and watch Him deliver us.

Are there any situations in your life today where you need that kind of "life"? Write out one place where you are needing God to move today.

_____

_____

_____

Continue to trust the Lord with your situation. Remember, He has promised you that *"if you thirst and if you believe on Him,"* you will be filled with the Spirit of God.

If you are suffering, you can be assured that the Lord is close. He knows the struggles you are facing. He has great plans for your life in spite of those trials. To tell you the truth, our trials are a part of His plan. We only change through pain. I hate that, don't you? When we come through our present struggle, we find a renewed hope and trust in God. He finds us in our present darkness and brings much needed light.

No matter where you are today, let me remind you: God loves you and God has a wonderful plan for your life. Have a blessed day and may the Word of God be your strength!

Read the proverb of the day and write in your journal.

Day Two

Today, let's take a closer look at our memory verse.

Write out Luke 14:26.

_____

_____

I can already hear your response, "Great, now I have to give up my family to follow Jesus." In this verse, Jesus is not asking us to stop loving our family. The second commandment is to love them as ourselves. He also said they would know we were His disciples by our love for each other. Yet, He requires that we never love anyone *more* than we love Him. Why do you think Jesus would tell us this? He knows that if we haven't put Him first, we wouldn't be able to be obedient to what He tells us. Ask the Lord today to show you any place that you might struggle with putting Him first.

1. Is there anyone in your life you would rather please than Him?

2. What about your own life? Have you surrendered your dreams and plans to Jesus?

He requires you to do that if you are going to be His disciple. Jesus is looking for soldiers but He is looking for "Surrendered Soldiers." To be "surrendered" means that you have given up possession of your own life. It also means that you have given up control of what He chooses to do with you. Know this though, Jesus will never take you anywhere or ask you to do anything without giving you the grace to accomplish the task. I love that about the Lord. He asks us to be **righteous** and then He supplies the **righteousness** we need. Are you living the crucified life? You may be able to nail your feet to the cross and even one of your hands, but it will take someone else to nail your final hand. God may allow pain in your life. Are you willing to be crucified even if it means suffering loss? Now I realize that you probably won't be crucified on a cross, but as you surrender your life to the Lord, it may feel like death. Remember, He can be trusted to resurrect all that He has planned for your life. He wants to walk you through the cross... death to you, so you can live the rest of your life alive in Him.

Read the memory verses to yourself before going on. Read John 8 and answer the following questions:

1. Why do you think Jesus offered them the opportunity to stone the woman in verse 7?

2. It is so exciting when Jesus forgives us our sins! When Jesus forgave this woman in verse 11, He also gave her a command. What was it?

3. In verse 31, how does Jesus say we can tell we are His disciples?

4. In verse 32, what does Jesus mean by the truth setting you free?

5. In verse 44, what does Jesus say the devil is?

6. In verse 47, who hears God's words?

7. Can you hear God as you read your Bible? He is speaking to you today. Will you obey?

We are living our lives in a very troubled world. You need to be able to hear God as you study and as you live out your day. If you are struggling with hearing Him, pray and ask Him to speak to you. To simply read the words will only produce an academic fathead. You should be changing as you read and meditate on the Word of God. It has life in it and it will produce life in you. Reading and studying the Word of God changed my life. Reading the Word of God opened the door for me to have an intimate relationship with the Lord.

Read the proverb of the day and write in your journal.

Day Three

Write out Matthew 16:24.

_____

_____

_____

_____

In this verse, Jesus explained to His disciples the "absolute cost" of discipleship. We discovered this week, as He suffered, we too must be willing to suffer. To be a disciple is to come after Him, to follow Him. We must follow as a sheep would follow his shepherd or as a soldier would follow his captain. Our aim must be the same as our Master's and that is to do the will of the Father. That is why Bible study is so important!

Notice in this verse that it is by choice, *"If any man or woman would come after Me."* Think about that today. Let me ask you a question? Do you follow after Christ? You may simply be following Him because your friends do or your spouse does. I am praying that as you learn about true "discipleship", you will want to follow Jesus just to know Him.

The first and most difficult lesson is to die to yourself. Once you have truly experienced death to self, following Jesus will become the joy of your life. Even in times of difficulty, you will experience His faithfulness. Remember, to find your life you must first be willing to lose it, to give it up. If you try to save your life in this world, you will lose it for all eternity. People are searching for all kinds of things to meet the need in their lives; drugs, alcohol, sexual addiction, popularity and acceptance. Jesus Himself has promised to supply all we need.

As you ponder this verse, you will see that the exchange of your will brings you the very blessings of heaven. However, as it is written: *"But as it is written, Eye hath not seen, nor ear heard, neither have entered into the heart of man, the things which God hath prepared for them that love them."* **(1 Corinthians 2:9)**

What is the life that Jesus is dreaming with you? Do you lay in bed and wonder what wonderful and exciting things He has planned for you? Knowing and following Him brings a peace that nothing else can supply. His presence around us, protecting us and directing us is an immeasureable joy.

Maybe today that seems far away to you. Please believe me when I tell you that all He is asking from you today is your heart's absolute commitment. Can you follow Him today? Can you trust Him? I pray that this day will be life-changing as you move with Him through your studies of the book of John.

Read John, Chapter 9.

1. Write out one thing that you have learned from the story of Jesus healing the blind man.

2. What did the blind man believe about Jesus after he was healed?

3. Many believers walk in spiritual blindness. This blind man received spiritual sight as well as physical sight. In what area are you still spiritually blind? (Hint: Any place in your life where you just can't see it the way Jesus sees it, you are spiritually blind.)

4. In verse 31, we learn who God hears. Are you qualified to hear?

5. Why does Jesus say He came into the world in verse 39?

6. Why did the Pharisees remain in sin?

7. Whose disciple did the Pharisees claim to be in verse 28?

8. Had there ever been another blind man who had his sight restored?

9. The blind man did what two things in verse 38?

10. Have you asked the Lord to heal your blindness? Do you have the faith to ask for healing today?

Read the proverb of the day and write in your journal.

Day Four

If you are going to be a disciple of Jesus, you must understand "grace." Grace is God doing for you what you cannot do for yourself. Grace is *"undeserved favor or the undeserved blessing of God."* As we study discipleship, it is important for you to see that Jesus is the one who will conform you to His image. It is not something you do for yourself. Yes, you will continue to make mistakes. Peter failed when he denied Christ, as did the other disciples, but they received God's forgiveness and His mercy. It is very important for you to forgive yourself for things you have done in the past that have grieved the heart of God. He died on Calvary so you could have a second chance and a third and a fourth, if necessary. If you will be willing to die to yourself, He will be faithful to finish what He has started in you.

Today, instead of reading your chapter in John, I would like you to write out a prayer on a separate piece of paper (so you can throw it away). In this prayer, I would like you to identify any "secret memories" that you might have. A "secret memory" is something in your mind or in your heart that you wouldn't want anyone else to know about. We are so ashamed of our sin. We even try to hide it from God while the enemy just keeps bringing it up. It may be something that you have struggled with for a long time and each time you attempt to live for Jesus—there it is, haunting you!

Let's settle it once and for all. I don't care how bad it is, Jesus died so you could be free! Do you want to be free? Today, I want you to give it to Jesus. Punishing or thinking less of yourself will not make you a disciple. It is okay that you have failed. That makes you a candidate for God's grace. (We will talk more about that tomorrow.) Now, be honest with yourself and with your Lord. Then mark these two verses in your Bible, Psalm 103:12 & 13, *"...As far as the east is from the west, so far hath he removed our transgressions from us. Like as a father pitieth his children, so the Lord pitieth them that fear him."*

After you have done your assignment, turn to 1 John 1:9. I want you to draw a little cross right by the verse. Place a small reminder of what has happened today (M.S.M.). That's to remind the devil that all your sins, even your secret memory, have been forgiven.

MY SECRET MEMORY   FORGIVEN

If the memory of this sin continues to haunt you, remember that Satan condemns, Jesus brings conviction. Don't allow the enemy to keep taking you back there.

For the last several years, I have done a considerable amount of counseling. Now, granted, the majority of the people who come to me have been deeply wounded. The result of the pain they carry is continual wrong choices. The thing that amazes me is the inability they have to forgive themselves for their own personal sin.

I, too, struggled the same way. Hiding my sin from myself was an altogether too familiar pattern. I did discover, however, that until I allowed the Lord to cleanse every hidden memory, I could never overcome the sin patterns I had built.

Studying sovereignty was the key for me. God, who created me, was the only one who could deliver me from my painful past and bring me hope for an overcoming future.

He created you, as well. He knows every sin that was committed against you and every willful sin you have committed. By bringing these memories to the Creator, you are allowing Him to free you. That freedom comes as you forgive others, forgive yourself and assume personal responsibility for your choices.

You may find it painful but I can testify to you that it will be worth it. Romans 8:28 testifies to the sovereignty of God by declaring that all things work together for the good of those who love God. That is an absolute you can believe in. When you begin to stand upon the absolutes of God, you will notice a new stability in your life. The Word of God equips you to withstand the storms of life. Simply becoming aware of God's absolutes, however, will not make you an overcomer. You must believe them. The power in believing the absolutes of God is found in receiving them into your very heart and making them your truth.

The Lord is aware of every secret memory that haunts you. By acknowledging them to the Lord and taking responsibility where you need to, the Lord will heal your memories. I quote from *Prisoner of Hope*, *"Maybe you feel like you have had your hope deferred, living in a prison in your own circumstances. Whether you are struggling with your present circumstances or unresolved circumstances from the past, the truth is that you need to be delivered from your chains. Would you be willing to begin by accepting Romans 8:28 as your foundational absolute?"*

Romans 8:28 says, *"And we know that all things work together for good to them that love God, to them who are the called according to His purpose."*

Heavenly Father,

I pray that as we bring these memories to You, that You would bring healing to the damaged places in our hearts. I pray that You would teach our hearts to fear Your name. As we bring You the pain of these memories, I pray that You would release us from the pain and guilt we bear. I love You and I thank You for healing us! In Jesus name, Amen.

Read the proverb of the day and write in your journal.

Day Five

Today, we will study John, Chapter 10. If you are a believer in Jesus Christ, this chapter will strongly confirm this. Read the whole chapter and then we will look at some specific passages.

1. In verse 4, how does Jesus say that the sheep know to follow Him?

2. In verse 5, why won't they follow the voice of a stranger?

3. What does verse 9 say to you?

4. What does the thief come for in verse 10?

5. What does Jesus come for in verse 10?

Read John 10: 27-29 and answer these questions:

1. According to these verses, are you a Christian?

2. Do you hear His voice? (You can hear Him through Bible study, preaching, music, etc.)

3. Do you follow Him? (Remember, a disciple is a follower.)

4. What does He give to you?

5. Can you be taken from the hand of God?

6. Do you understand that verses 28 and 29 are a covenant promise to you that you can't lose your salvation? A rhema is scripture that God has made personal to you. Is this a rhema? Mark it in your Bible with a capital R.

Write these verses out IF you believe they are true, John 10:27-29.

_____

_____

_____

_____

_____

_____

_____

_____

_____

Write out a prayer thanking the Lord for the assurance you have of your salvation.

Dear Jesus,

_____

_____

_____

_____

_____

_____

_____

_____

Read the proverb of the day and write in your journal.

Day Six

OSWALD CHAMBERS

*"If any man come to Me and hate not...
he cannot be my disciple."*

If the closest relationships of life clash with the claims of Jesus Christ, He says it must be instant obedience to Himself. Discipleship means personal, passionate devotion to a person, our Lord Jesus Christ. There is a difference between devotion to a person and devotion to principles or to a cause. Our Lord never proclaimed a cause; He proclaimed personal devotion to Himself. To be a disciple is to be a devoted love-slave of the Lord Jesus. Many of us who call ourselves Christians are not devoted to Jesus Christ. No man on earth has this passionate love to the Lord Jesus unless the Holy Ghost has imparted it to him. We may admire Him, we may respect Him and reverence Him, but we cannot love Him. The only Lover of the Lord Jesus is the Holy Ghost, and He sheds abroad the very love of God in our hearts. Whenever the Holy Ghost sees a chance of glorifying Jesus, He will take your heart, your nerves, your whole personality, and simply make you blaze and glow with devotion to Jesus Christ.

The Christian life is stamped by "moral spontaneous originality," consequently the disciple is open to the same charge that Jesus Christ was, that of inconsistency. But Jesus Christ was always consistent to God, and the Christian must be consistent to the life of the Son of God in him, not consistent to hard and fast creeds. Men pour themselves into creeds and God has to blast them out of their prejudices before they can become devoted to Jesus Christ.

*(Oswald Chambers, July 2nd)

Today, I want to backtrack a little. So far, we have discovered that to be a disciple we must die to ourselves, put Jesus first in everything and be willing to suffer for His sake. It should help us to realize the Lord doesn't allow suffering unless it is to glorify Him. We have read about men giving their lives up to follow Christ and we've read about miracles. Now let's look at the secret to Jesus' ministry.

John 10:30 says, *"I and my Father are one."* Jesus knew oneness with His Father was the ultimate goal! Jesus stayed focused on the reason He was here. We should be one with our Heavenly Father as well.

Read John 10:30-40.

1. Why were these religious men threatening to stone Jesus?

2. Do you believe Jesus enjoyed the persecution He was enduring?

3. Why was He faithful?

4. After Jesus left "this" crowd, He found a "different" group. Did they believe?

As we finish today, let me remind you of Romans 8:28. No matter what following Jesus costs you, I can promise it will all work together for your good! Stay faithful to the course, O mighty follower of Jesus. No matter what you are going through today, can you accept it as a part of God's eternal purpose for your life? Following Jesus should be exciting even though, at times, it will be difficult to understand. Please do not allow the enemy to sidetrack you by his taunts such as, *"Why do you want to follow Jesus? Why do you want to give everything up?"* Don't even answer him. Simply reaffirm yourself with these words, *"Today my Savior is working everything in my life for good because I love him and because I have been called according to His purpose."*

Write out your memory verses here.

_____

_____

_____

_____

Read the proverb of the day and write in your journal.

Day Seven

When the Lord walked upon the earth, He spent quite a bit of time teaching on "commitment." He was committed to fulfilling His Father's plan for the Kingdom. People today are committed to bodybuilding, bodysculpting and bodyworship. Physical exercise is important but making it your first priority is wrong. Jesus has called us out to be servants to the body of Christ. In order to do that, we must have a "love commitment" to Him above all else. If we truly are one of His sheep like we read about in John 10, we will have His passion for other sheep. We will share His commitment to the body of Christ.

Read John 11 and answer the following questions:

1. What type of sickness does verse 4 say Lazarus had? In other words, what was the "purpose" for his sickness?

2. How did Jesus feel about Martha, Mary and Lazarus?

3. After Lazarus had died and Jesus had received the word of his death, He tells His disciples that He is glad He was not there so that they might believe. What do you think He meant?

4. If you witnessed someone being raised from the dead, would it make you a better believer?

5. Verse 35 is the shortest verse in the Bible. What do you think it means?

6. In verse 44, after Jesus calls Lazarus out of the grave, He tells the people to loose the grave clothes. All around you are believers bound in sin.

   a) Have you been loosed from your grave clothes?

   b) Are you ready to loose the grave clothes of others?

Now, that is the heart of Jesus.

Read the proverb of the day and write in your journal.

The Beginning of Discipleship
Month One - Week Three

Week Three Checklist

To keep track of how consistent you are becoming in your walk as a disciple, check off your work on this chart as you go. You will either be encouraged as you see your progress or challenged as you see your inconsistency. I am praying that you will be the *"workman that needeth not be ashamed."*

	Bible Study	Memory	Proverbs	Prayer
Sunday	_____	_____	_____	_____
Monday	_____	_____	_____	_____
Tuesday	_____	_____	_____	_____
Wednesday	_____	_____	_____	_____
Thursday	_____	_____	_____	_____
Friday	_____	_____	_____	_____
Saturday	_____	_____	_____	_____

Prayer Requests

_____

_____

_____

_____

_____

Memory Verses
Month One - Week Three

John 13:35
*"By this shall all men know that ye are my disciples,
if ye have love one to another."*

1 Corinthians 13:13
*"And now abideth faith, hope, charity, these three;
but the greatest of these is charity."*

PROVERBS JOURNAL

Proverbs Chapter _____ _____

_____

Proverbs Chapter _____ _____

_____

Proverbs Chapter _____ _____

_____

Proverbs Chapter _____ _____

_____

Proverbs Chapter _____ _____

_____

Proverbs Chapter _____ _____

_____

Proverbs Chapter _____ _____

_____

The Beginning of Discipleship
Month One - Week Three

Day One

Your memory verses for this week are:

John 13:35   *"By this shall all men know that ye are my disciples, if ye have love one to an-other."*

1 Corinthians 13:13   *"And now abideth faith, hope, charity, these three; but the greatest of these is charity."*

The focus of our study this week will be "love." Turn to 1 Corinthians, Chapter 13, and read it out lord. A disciple is easily recognized by His love for the brethren. I am not talking about the world's kind of love. God's love is centered around forgiveness—always assuming the best. His love is like a river that has an endless supply of water. This love requires death to yourself. It not only forgives offences but gives a second chance and a third, if necessary. Love like God's love is unattainable without living the crucified life. But, as we allow Him to, the Father can love others through us and they will then know we are His disciples. Have you ever noticed how easy it is to love those who love you? God's love calls us to love even our enemies.

1 Corinthians 13:13   *"And now abideth faith, hope, charity, these three; but the greatest of these is charity."*

Love has many faces, many facets to it. Few people have explored all the depths and heights of love. Ephesians 3:17-19 says, *"That Christ may dwell in your hearts by faith; that ye, being rooted and grounded in love, may be able to comprehend with all saints what is the breadth, and length, and depth, and height; and to know the love of Christ, which passeth knowledge, that ye might be filled with all the fullness of God."* Faith produces love. Love is the action of faith. Without love, faith has no feelings. Jesus exemplified the action of love by His death on the cross. John 15:13 states that, *"No greater love hath no man than this, that a man lay down his life for his friends."*

That love could be expressed by mere words seems impossible. Through the expressions of our thoughts, we come to see our own hearts. Love can be held in your hand, love can be sung, love can be written, love can be seen in the expression of the eyes and love can be heard through caring words or even, sometimes, through words of correction.

Please write out and memorize your memory verses.

_____
_____
_____
_____
_____
_____
_____
_____
_____
_____
_____
_____

I know that many of you are wondering how you will ever be able to love the way the Lord intended. If you have been deeply wounded, it may take time. The Lord works in time. Each day that you surrender and seek Him, He will work in your heart to bring the necessary healing.

To find yourself in the place where you can't forgive is to give up. Please don't. Just tell the Lord you know you must forgive but that you are struggling. You need His help.

Honestly, during those times when I couldn't forgive was when I came to know the Lord more intimately. Many times I have experienced His love in such a way that I was overcome to choose against my emotions.

Love comes from Him. He is the fountain of love. Trust Him to flow through you and fill you with His love—unconditional love.

Read the proverb of the day and write in your journal.

Day Two

BOUNDLESS... Love has no limits.
EXHILARATING... Love motivates the heart.
INFLUENCING... Love changes the direction of your life.
FULFILLING... Love satisfies a need.

In receiving love, we equip ourselves to be givers of love. Never will you meet a man or a woman who has a great capacity to love who has not first learned to receive love. *"We love Him because He first loved us."*

Love never seeks to protect itself. Love is vulnerable. Love takes risks. Was it not love that compelled Peter to walk on the water?

In love, you will find compassion, acts of kindness, patience and endurance. Through love, you will come to know disappointment, disillusionment and despair. Because of love, you will possess joy, peace and delight. Psalms 37:4 says, *"Delight thyself also in the Lord: and he shall give thee the desires of thine heart."*

Embrace love as a child. Welcome love as a friend. Receive love that you might become one who loves. Faith, hope and love, the greatest of these is love.

Read John 12:1-25 and answer the following questions:

1. In verse 3, we find the story of Mary anointing Jesus' feet. Would you be comfortable with doing something like that? If not, why not?

2. Let's take a closer look at verses 24 and 25. Here is another reminder that we must die to find life. Are you bearing fruit in your life? In what area or areas? Give an example.

3. If you were witnessing to an unbeliever, what is one thing you learned about light and darkness from this chapter?

4. a) Why were the rulers, who believed in Jesus, not willing to confess Him as Savior?

   b) Is it possible to be "religious" and not know the Lord Jesus as Savior?

   c) Would you call them "disciples"? Why or why not?

5. How did Jesus know what He was to speak?

6. How can we know what to speak?

The whole world seems to be walking in darkness. Have you noticed it? They are piercing and tattooing every inch of their bodies, seeking identity in anything other than Jesus. Following Jesus, however, requires a loss of identity. You become His and no longer serve yourself. They are few and far between who are willing to follow. The bad news is that, in the end of our earthly lives, we will begin our eternal life. It will be too late for change then.

I don't believe a tattoo or a body piercing will send you to hell. I do believe not surrendering your life to Jesus qualifies you for hell. How much do you know about hell? Do you believe it exists today? In John 12, they refused the light that would have rescued them from an eternity in hell. What about you? Are you responding to the light the Lord is giving to you?

As we await the second coming of the Lord, it's only going to get darker. We must know the Word of God to maintain holiness as we await His return. Remember, we were chosen for this time. I pray that you will continue to give yourself to His Word. Knowing that, as you make the Word of God a priority in your life, you are positioning yourself for a consistent overcoming life. Nothing you do on a daily basis will be as important in the days to come as reading and meditating upon the Word of God!

Read the proverb of the day and write in your journal.

Day Three

Write out John 13:35.

_____

_____

_____

_____

_____

Read John, Chapter 13. Answer the following questions:

1. In verses 1-15, what example of love is Jesus showing us?

2. When Jesus says to *"wash one another's feet,"* He is saying to serve one another. List several ways you could serve someone in your life today.

3. Did Jesus know who would betray Him?

4. Did Jesus wash the feet of the one who would betray Him?

5. Could you have done that? Why or why not?

6. In verse 34, Jesus gives us a new commandment, what is it?

7. What was the purpose in this commandment?

8. As you have studied "discipleship," how important do you think "love" is?

9. Do you think it's possible to be a disciple without God's love?

Do you understand that love is a picture of grace? Remember earlier this week when we studied how much we need grace to walk in discipleship? Grace not only empowers us to accomplish the purposes of our life, but it gives us the faith to continue when we make mistakes. God wants us to operate in that kind of "grace-love" with others.

Do you feel you can love others in the way He loves you? Think about those whom you struggle with loving and forgiving. Have they done anything to you that would compare to your mistakes in your walk with the Lord?

How easily we expect Him to forgive us, but we don't want to forgive others and give them another chance. Think about it. Who do you need to forgive today? If today was the last opportunity you had to be free from your unforgiveness, would it be easier to choose? Every day you hang on to unforgiveness is another day you surrend to the enemy's plans. Choose to forgive. Choose…today.

FORGIVENESS

Forgiveness is a gift You have given me.
A cleansed past You lovingly bought.
I choose today to love as You do,
Living out the message You have taught.

I cannot love the way You love
Unless my heart has accepted grace.
May I open my life to Your tender care
And forgive allowing You my pain to embrace.

Forgiveness is a wonderful thing.
It lifts me above life's sorrow.
Because of Your love, Jesus,
I hopefully embrace my tomorrow.

Read the proverb of the day and write in your journal.

Day Four

We have been looking at how love affects our relationship with Christ. We have discovered that we have to love and forgive ourselves before we can be what God has called us to be. We have also discovered that we are required to love and forgive others. Today's reading in John will bring us more truth on the subject of "God's love." God's love is nothing like man's love. Most people struggle with accepting that. As we were growing up, we knowingly or unknowingly began to frame our belief system based on how we were treated.

If our authorities were consistent in displaying God's love to us by balancing correction and using wisdom and affirmation, we grew up with a correct view of love.

More likely, however, there were inconsistent methods of correction and love shown to you. It is important to remember that our authorities had damaged authorities raising them. How far back do you think this goes? It goes clear back to Adam and Eve. Now, you have the opportunity to change all that by forgiving those who hurt you and by embracing God's love. His love will heal and restore you where you have been damaged. Expect to be loved today as you walk alongside your Savior.

Read John 14 and answer the following questions:

1. What is Jesus talking about in the first six verses?

2. Write out verse 12. (This verse is a promise that we can be "disciples".) You may want to mark it as a rhema in your Bible (R).

3. When you received Jesus as Savior, you also received the Comforter, the Holy Spirit. How long has the Holy Spirit promised to stay in your life? (Look closely at verses 16 and 17.)

4. Beginning in verse 21, how can you know if you truly love Jesus?

5. In verse 26, what will the Holy Spirit do for you?

Maybe you haven't realized how important the Holy Spirit is in your life. Did you know He is the third person of the Trinity? Did you know the Holy Spirit is the voice of God at work in your life? I talk to so many believers who aren't walking in daily fellowship with the Spirit of God. Why would we do that? Why would we ask someone to forgive our sin and then give them full control of our life and not want to hear from Him daily? Well, most of the time it is because we don't want to be responsible. The Spirit of God is going to teach us the ways of the Father and then He is going to remind us when we don't keep them.

Now, depending on your motive, avoiding the voice of God in your life would make sense if you weren't striving to please the Father. However, if you have made it your passion to follow Him and to know Him, you must have fellowship with the Holy Spirit. I have been saved for nearly twenty years and I know that the Holy Spirit has been grieved with me so many times. Whether I acted in ignorance, stubbornness or just simple rebellion to His voice, He has always forgiven me when I repented of my own way. I need the Holy Spirit's comfort when I fail and I need His reassurance when I am on track. If you aren't listening to Him and maintaining your relationship to Him, you will miss it. Remember, just reading your Bible will produce a legalistic fat-head. You need the Spirit to teach you how to apply the teachings of the Bible to your own life in such a way that Jesus Christ is being glorified, not your works.

Dear Holy Spirit,

Forgive me for not yielding to You. Forgive me for ignoring Your voice and Your direction in my life. I need You and I long to be in fellowship with You. I pray that You'd give me a renewed awareness of Your presence at work in my life. I need Your help everyday to accomplish all the Father has for me. Open my eyes to all You want me to see. Fill me, Holy Spirit, until there is nothing left of me and my selfish plans. Order my steps and glorify Your name. In Jesus name, Amen.

Read the proverb of the day and write in your journal.

Day Five

Abiding in Christ. The Lord wants you to abide in Him every day. To abide is to trust. You cannot ever hope to follow if you don't choose to abide and you sure won't be willing to pay the price in times of suffering.

There is a very important verse in today's passage. Let's look at John 16:13 which reads, *"Howbeit when he, the Spirit of truth, is come, he will guide you into all truth: for he shall not speak of himself; but whatsoever he shall hear, that shall he speak: and he will shew you things to come."* Abiding in Chrsit includes studying your Bible, praying, maintaining an attitude of prayer and embracing what the Holy Spirit shows you. Most believers wander through each day oblivious to what the Spirit is showing them. I have found the Spirit of Truth, the Comforter, to be my friend. When I listen, He is constantly speaking to me; park here, let's go over there, let's talk to this person, eat this, rest awhile, not to mention He is constantly preparing me for what lies ahead. So many times He has spoken a word to me just before I needed it. Do you know the Holy Spirit like that? I hope so.

Imagine you are a branch on a giant oak tree. The Holy Spirit is not only the trunk of the tree but is the root system of the tree. You get all your nourishment from the tree's root system because you are attached to the tree. The roots, deep in the soil, bring nourishment to the branch. But if you, the branch, tried to live separate from the tree, you would die for lack of nourishment. Just like the tree supplies nourishment to the branch, the Lord knows how to bring everything to you that you need. Be a branch today. Abide. Trust Him to provide all your needs.

Read John 15 and answer the following questions:

1. Let's look at verse 2. What does Jesus do to the branch that does not bear fruit?

2. What does He do to the branch that bears fruit?

3. How can the Father be glorified in your life?

4. Write out John 15:12.

_____

_____

_____

5. List three ways God loves you.

a)

b)

c)

6. Do you love like that?

7. How can we know we are the friend of God?

8. Did you choose God or did God choose you?

I believe it is so important to realize that God chose us —we did not choose Him. We had the option to respond to Him or go our own way. However, He drew us to Himself. If He could choose us, then I'm convinced He alone can change us. Aren't you grateful? Our responsibility is to love and obey Him. He does the rest. I have found that He has an amazing ability to create circumstances in my life that teach me what He is presently wanting me to learn. With that in mind, I get up everyday, anxious to see what I am going to live out. It is a great adventure—following Him.

Read the proverb of the day and write in your journal.

Day Six

I hope that by now you have come to realize that following Jesus will separate you from everything but His sovereign plan for your life. You see, the Lord planned every day of your life before you were even born. The Psalmist says that, *"The steps of a good man are ordered by the Lord: and He delighteth in his way."* (Psalms 37:23) Wow! You may be like I was and find that some days of your life are not very Godly. You ask yourself, *"Where am I and why am I acting like this?"* Good question. You are in process. The Lord is allowing you to fail to expose your heart to you. He already knows what is in your heart. He wants to remove it. Remember, His heart toward you is redemptive. The Holy Spirit convicts you of your mistakes and offers you a way of escape from them. He turns your failures into opportunities to receive His love and His forgiveness. When we truly believe that we are loved and forgiven, we long to please Him. Don't you think? I want to encourage you today. Don't quit because you failed. I have covenanted with Jesus that I will never quit trying…never. On the last day of my life, I will arise and believe I can be free. Will you also believe?

So, you want to be a warrior?
There is a price that you must pay.
If to follow in God's army,
A disciple you wish to stay.

Being His disciple,
A call that you must hear.
For though many seek to follow,
Only a few will to His heart stay dear.

He has called you to be His disciple.
The road of excellence you see.
Make hearing His voice your priority,
And then you will stay free.

Read John 16 and answer the following questions:

1. When the Comforter has come, what will He do?

2. When the Spirit of Truth has come, what will He do?

3. a) What does verse 23 say?

   b) Is that a promise or not? (Mark an R by that verse in your Bible.)

4. Why does the Father love you? (v. 27)

5. a) What will we find in the world?

   b) How are we to handle this?

Please pray with me.

Holy Spirit,

Thank You for Your presence in my life. I need You to guide me and teach me the ways of Jesus Christ. I long to meet with You daily as we seek to glorify the Father. Keep me sensitive to Your voice. Keep me aware of how deeply I need You in my everyday decisions. Thank You for forgiving me for all the times I haven't been sensitive to You. In Jesus name, Amen.

Read the proverb of the day and write in your journal.

Day Seven

Write out your memory verses.

John 13:35

_____

_____

_____

_____

1 Corinthians 13:13

_____

_____

_____

_____

The world has many concepts of love today, but we are talking about the love of God. It's a love you may sometimes have a difficult time comprehending. I have found that so many times we put our expectations of God on how we've been treated in the past by our friends, our parents and other authorities. That is why studying the Word is so important to gain the truth. Your heavenly Father loves you. He sees you inside and out. Kind of scary, huh? He longs to love you to His side, to overcome. Will you let Him love you?

1. What is love according to God's Word?

Ask the Lord to show you someone toward whom you can extend love. Make a card, write a letter, or make a phone call to let that someone know that Jesus loves them. Do you know the Word says that love will cover a multitude of sins? There are so many people in your sphere of influence that are hurting. They need the love of Jesus today. Many people are so wounded they can't find the courage to begin again. I know. I was like that. The Lord brought people in my life to speak to me and to heal me. I heard their love for God and it gave me the courage and the strength to respond to God myself. Can you love like that?

Read the proverb of the day and write in your journal.

The Beginning of Discipleship
Month One - Week Four

Week Four Checklist

To keep track of how consistent you are becoming in your walk as a disciple, check off your work on this chart as you go. You will either be encouraged as you see your progress or challenged as you see your inconsistency. I am praying that you will be the *"workman that needeth not be ashamed."*

	Bible Study	**Memory**	**Proverbs**	**Prayer**
Sunday	_____	_____	_____	_____
Monday	_____	_____	_____	_____
Tuesday	_____	_____	_____	_____
Wednesday	_____	_____	_____	_____
Thursday	_____	_____	_____	_____
Friday	_____	_____	_____	_____
Saturday	_____	_____	_____	_____

Prayer Requests

_____

_____

_____

_____

_____

_____

Memory Verses
Month One - Week Four

Ephesians 4:32 *"And be ye kind one to another, tenderhearted, forgiving one another, even as God for Christ's sake hath forgiven you."*

Colossians 3:13 *"Forbearing one another, and forgiving one another, if any man have a quarrel against any: even as Christ for- gave you, so also do ye."*

PROVERBS JOURNAL

Proverbs Chapter _____ _____

_____

Proverbs Chapter _____ _____

_____

Proverbs Chapter _____ _____

_____

Proverbs Chapter _____ _____

_____

Proverbs Chapter _____ _____

_____

Proverbs Chapter _____ _____

_____

Proverbs Chapter _____ _____

_____

A DISCIPLE
One who willingly forgives!

The Beginning of Discipleship
Month One - Week Four

Day One

Ephesians 4:32	*"And be ye kind one to another, tenderhearted, forgiving one another, even as God for Christ's sake hath forgiven you."*
Colossians 3:13	*"Forbearing one another, and forgiving one another, if any man have a quarrel against any: even as Christ forgave you, so also do ye."*

"Discipleship." The road is narrow, the rewards eternal. So many people live their lives filled with bitterness. Living with unforgiveness gives the enemy a door to your heart. This week's focus will be on forgiveness. We have already discovered that to live a crucified life, we must be willing to die to ourselves. That includes always forgiving those who hurt us. As you follow Him in discipleship, there will be many opportunities to forgive. Our verses this week will focus on that. Please list the people you need to forgive, even if you are not yet ready to forgive them.

The People I Need To Forgive:

1.

2.

3.

4.

5.

6.

Read John 17 and answer the following questions:

1. a) In verse 14, what had knowing the Word produced in their lives?

   b) Do you realize that if you live the Word, you will face rejection and persecution?

2. a) What did John say would be the answer to the world hating them?

    b) Should Jesus take them out of the world? Why or why not?

3. How are we to be sanctified?

4. In verses 21-23, what has Jesus prayed for us? List each thing.

    a)

    b)

    c)

Beginning today, pray for the person or persons, by name, whom you've listed as people you need to forgive. Pray for them every day this week. At the end of the week, we'll see if you feel differently toward them.

Write out your memory verses.

_____
_____
_____
_____
_____
_____

Read the proverb of the day and write in your journal.

Day Two

"**Forgiveness**" It's just one word, but it can be difficult to live if you are not dead to yourself. Many times a day, you have the opportunity to forgive or harbor an offense. To harbor an offense is to give it a place to rest inside your heart. In other words, a home. It will not only rest there, but it will grow into bitterness and resentment if left there. The measure of forgiveness that Jesus requires is for you to forgive as He has forgiven you. Your verse in Ephesians talks about that kind of forgiveness.

Think about the people you have put on your list to pray for this week. Write down what they have done to hurt you (on a separate piece of paper). Is what they have done worse than how you have treated Jesus in the past? Are you asking Him to forgive you for something you are not willing to forgive others for? The Bible says, *"that with the measure of forgiveness you forgive, you shall be forgiven."* To be a disciple, we must learn to walk in forgiveness. I cannot stress this enough. That's why I keep going over it. We don't forgive because we think they don't deserve our forgiveness. We must forgive because God has commanded us to forgive.

The bitterness and lack of forgiveness act as an anchor in your life, anchoring you to your past in a negative way. As you are reading through Proverbs, I trust that you can see how important it is for your heart to be set upon the ways of God's heart. Continue to ask the Lord to give you a heart to forgive that you might become a man or woman of wisdom. Forgiveness is not only a decision, but it is also a process whereby we must choose daily to forgive. The challenge is not to forgive and forget. The real honor comes in one's ability to forgive and still remember.

Let's face it, everyone has something to forgive. Too many times we think we are the only one who has been hurt. Oh, how I wish I could have learned earlier in my Christian life that being angry only hurts me. We think by carrying an offense, locking onto our anger, that we are making "them" pay. In reality, we become poisoned by our own wrong emotions. If you walk with the Lord long enough you will discover, as I have, that He won't allow you to harbor unforgiveness. It will affect your relationship with Him. I have found that it is much easier to forgive quickly and not risk losing fellowship with the Lord.

Read John, Chapter 18.

In verse 10-11, Peter experienced the difficulty of discipleship. God's ways are not like our ways. Jesus was willing to drink from the cup His father had given to Him.

MONTH ONE — WEEK FOUR

1. Is there anything in your life right now that you are struggling with, a cup you don't want to drink from? If so, write out a prayer asking the Lord to give you the faith to know it will accomplish its desired purpose.

   _____

   _____

2. In what three verses did Peter deny Jesus?

   a)

   b)

   c)

3. If you had been Peter, would you have denied Christ?

4. Is there any place in your life where you are denying Christ?

5. How would things have been different if Jesus' kingdom had been of this world?

6. Who called Jesus a king?

7. Why did Jesus say that He came into the world?

8. Who hears the voice of the Lord?

9. What question did Pilate ask in verse 38?

10. Who did Pilate release?

Read the proverb of the day and write in your journal.

Day Three

"Forgiveness"

F - orgetting that it ever happened

O - only expecting the best

R - realizing that God has a redemptive heart

G - grace extended where it may not be deserved

I - inspired to overcome hurts and wounds

V - volitional love (love by your choice)

E - endless supply from God's heart

N - needing God's grace to accomplish it

E - expecting nothing in return

S - seeing God's love fulfilled

S - showing discipleship love

As you have prayed for those you struggle with forgiving, it is my prayer that God will make it very real to you that learning to forgive, as He forgives, is one of the most important lessons you will learn. To be honest, maybe we haven't truly understood His forgiveness. Maybe we have even taken it for granted. We thought because He was God that He should just forgive us. Now we see that He requires the same measure of forgiveness from us. Don't be discouraged if you don't feel like forgiving. All He requires from you is that you ask for His help. He will be faithful to change your feelings when the time is right. He is using this circumstance to conform you to His image.

The enemy would love to keep you as his prisoner, but my desire is to share with you that he always perverts the eternal sovereign plan of God. God wants to make you *a prisoner of hope*. God uses your mistakes and hurts to display His message of hope.

You have a decision to make. You have to decide whether you are going to allow these hurts and disappointments to dictate who you will be or whether you are going to allow the Word of God to show you who you are in Christ. At salvation, you inherited the right to have a sound mind and to walk out your life in wisdom. No matter how deeply you have been hurt, you still have that inheritance. You cannot trust your heart or feelings when you have been hurt. But, you can trust the Word of God. Don't be a prisoner of unforgiveness. Choose today to be *a prisoner of hope*.

Read John, Chapter 19.

1. As you read the story of the crucifixion, write out how it affected Pilate.

2. What did Jesus say to His mother as He was on the cross?

3. Who was involved in the burial of Jesus?

4. If you had been at the crucifixion of Christ, how do you think you would have felt?

5. Why do you think Pilate made the sign to hang above Jesus on the cross?

6. What language was it written in?

7. What were Jesus' final words on the cross?

8. Why didn't the soldiers break Jesus' legs?

9. Who did the priests claim was their king?

10. Why didn't the soldiers tear Jesus' coat?

Read the proverb of the day and write in your journal.

Day Four

There are times when the person you are struggling with is a person you really need in your life. God is waiting for you to be able to forgive them in order that He can give you "more than before." In other words, someone who is now your enemy could possibly be a very dear friend one day. Don't doubt God in this. He is bigger than you can imagine. Don't doubt what God is seeking to do in your life.

It is God who has allowed all the circumstances in our lives. His plans for us are good and not evil. Let me say it one more time: You have to decide today whether or not you are going to allow your past to dictate who you will be or whether you are going to allow the Word of God to show you who you are in Christ. Wisdom is you, the spirit man, the faith man, coming in agreement with God and His Word. I hope you can see the value of God's Word. You can't trust your heart or your feelings. You can trust the Word of God. If you are the ship and the Word of God is your anchor, you are now prepared to sail the ocean of life. You will weather the storms of life without losing your course. Remember, the purpose of an anchor is to make you steadfast, immovable, always abounding in the Lord.

How are you doing on your prayer time for the people you need to forgive? Write out your prayer for them today. One day, you will be able to look back at this journal and see how far you have come with them.

Dear Jesus, I ask You to bless...

_____

_____

_____

_____

_____

_____

_____

_____

_____

_____

_____

Read John, Chapter 20 and answer the following questions:

1. Who did Mary see at the tomb?

2. What question did they ask her?

3. When she saw Jesus, did she know it was Him?

4. What question did Jesus ask her?

5. What did Mary speak to Jesus at the tomb?

6. What name did Mary call Jesus?

7. What does the name mean?

8. Why couldn't Mary touch Him?

9. To whom did Jesus appear next?

10. What was their reaction?

Read the proverb of the day and write in your journal.

Day Five

Begin today by reading the words of the song, *"Table of Grace,"* by Phillips, Craig and Dean. Remember, as He has forgiven us, we need to forgive others.

TABLE OF GRACE

Hear the good news/You've been invited/
No matter what others may say/Your darkest sins/
Will be forgiven/And you will always have a place/
At the table of grace/The cup's never empty/
The plate's always full/And it's never too late/
To come and be filled/With love never ending/
You're always welcome at the table of grace/
So come you weak and heavy hearted/Don't try to hide
Your earthly scars/In His eyes, we are all equal/
Don't be afraid/Come as you are/
So let the first become the last/Let the poor put kings to shame/
Their willing hearts will be their treasure
By the power of Jesus name/
Everyone's welcome at the table of grace/

In review of what we have studied this past week, God is calling us to walk in forgiveness. As He has called us to a "table of grace" where we can be healed and forgiven, we should also be willing to prepare the same "table of grace" for those who have hurt us. Walking in forgiveness may be the single most important decision you make. Many, many people accept Jesus as their Lord and Savior, but never grow in their relationship to Him because of the pain in their hearts towards others. However, when we truly embrace walking in a daily lifestyle of forgiveness, the Lord can then use us to heal others. To quote from *A Prisoner of Hope*:

"God has a perfect plan for your life and until you can face the pain, forgive those who caused the pain, and face all your fears, you will never be willing to embrace it! In the book of Isaiah, the Lord calls us forth to be the one who

repairs the breach in our families. "And they that shall be of thee shall build the old waste places: thou shalt raise up the foundations of many generations; and thou shalt be called, The repairer of the breach, The restorer of paths to dwell in." (Isaiah 58:12) No matter how painful your past has been, God wants to use you to repair the breach. The ministry of hope is to build a bridge from your past to your future."

David says in Psalm 22:9 that hope was in his heart, even as he lay upon his mother's breast. *"But thou art He that took me out of the womb: thou didst make me hope when I was upon my mother's breasts."* If God was causing him to have hope that early in his life, then I believe every event he would encounter in his life would be God-ordained. Even our mistakes can be used by God to lay a foundation upon which hope can be built. Too many times we face our past and we forgive those who have hurt us, but then we stop. Facing our fears can be the most difficult step of all. We were created to be passionate and live our lives filled with hope. However, because we are afraid, we can't embrace the goodness of God. I have embraced His goodness and found it to be the healing point of my life. I could never walk in joy without my belief that each new day is worth living and experiencing.

Read John, Chapter 21 and answer the following questions:

1. a) When Jesus appeared to His disciples, He appeared in their everyday life. What were they doing?

   b) Are you looking for Him in your everyday life?

2. How many times did Jesus ask Peter if he loved him?

3. What did Jesus tell Peter to do?

4. How does that apply to your life?

5. In verse 21, Peter was very concerned about one of the other disciples. What was Jesus' response to that concern?

Read the proverb of the day and write in your journal.

Day Six

Congratulations! You have completed the book of John. I hope you are becoming more familiar with the life of Jesus Christ. Next week, we will look at some of the same stories as told from Mark's perspective. Today, read Matthew 18:21-35. Stop and read it now before you continue.

Herein lies the power of forgiveness. Remember, forgiveness is an act of repentance. It is realizing that being angry at the one who hurt you is wrong—it is sin. The power lies in choosing. Here is the doorway to true repentance—it is when we realize that no amount of punishment will repay what sin has caused. Remember also, he who needs forgiveness, easily bestows it. What is the worst thing you have ever done to shame the name of Christ? Imagine if Jesus treated you the way you are treating the one who has hurt you. I have met some incredible believers who have troubled pasts, but they walk at such levels of forgiveness. They realize what they have been forgiven for. They have such a level of gratefulness that they will not harbor bitterness. You and I must see ourselves undone before the Lord, to walk at that level of brokenness and forgiveness. Do you see yourself undone before the Lord?

In our passage in Matthew, verse 24, a man who owes $20 million is brought to the king. When the king requires payment, the servant begins to beg for forgiveness of the debt. Now, after being forgiven, this servant goes out and finds one of his fellow servants who owes $20 and demands payment. The fellow servant cannot pay and begins to beg. The forgiven servant shows no mercy and throws the debtor into prison.

How many times have we been like that, expecting God to forgive us but being so unwilling to forgive others? May the Lord open our hearts to forgive as we have been forgiven.

Please answer the following questions:

1. What was Peter's question to the Lord?

2. How did Jesus answer him?

3. How did the servant respond in verse 26?

4. How did the Lord of that servant respond?

5. What happens in verse 31?

6. What was the judgment against the forgiven servant?

7. Write out verse 35.

8. How does this story apply to your life?

9. What has Jesus specifically forgiven you for?

10. Who do you need to forgive?

Write out your memory verses for the week.

_____

_____

_____

_____

_____

_____

_____

Read the proverb of the day and write in your journal.

Day Seven

As we finish up this week, I would like you to list at least five things you've learned about discipleship.

1.

2.

3.

4.

5.

Have you forgiven those whom Jesus is showing you to forgive this week? If so, thank the Lord for showing you His forgiveness. If not, pray and then talk to someone close to you about it. Your walk with the Lord will not prosper until you have been able to forgive.

As we finish out our fourth week of discipleship, I trust that the Lord is speaking to you. Today, I would like you to read Psalms 42. This is one of my favorite Psalms. The psalmist identifies our need to be comforted. Webster's Dictionary defines comfort as, *"to soothe in time of grief or fear; to console; to ease physically; relieve; a state of ease; help or assistance."*

God is faithful to create these areas of need in our lives. He does that in order that we will seek Him out. He longs for His children to become so desperate for Him that they will stop everything else in their lives to find Him. Of course, all this time He has been as close as your next breath. We just think we have to search Him out. Revival is the process by which the Holy Spirit exposes our areas of need. He begins to fill the empty places with Himself. Oswald Chambers says, *"If you find a blank space in your life, don't hurry to fill it. Wait and let God come."*

Lets pray,

Lord Jesus, we need You more, more than we ever imagined. Our attempts at finding comfort in our lives leaves us hungrier than ever before. We ask You to give us revival. We need the fire of Your love to expose our hearts to its needs. Only Your presence can change the hopelessness of our lives. Don't change our circumstances, Lord, but change our focus. When we can see our circumstances through Your eyes of hope, we cannot be defeated. Make us lovers of You, Jesus, that we might become lovers of Your people. Prepare us for Your kingdom's work, Lord. In Jesus name, Amen.

Please list five areas in your life that you need the Lord to move in. By acknowledging your need, you are willingly looking to Him to be your source. I can promise you… He will be faithful.

1.

2.

3.

4.

5.

Read the proverb of the day and write in your journal.

PSALMS 42

This one thing I know.
No other comfort will I seek.
All other places that I have tried,
Have only proved to be weak.

Pleasure for a moment.
Comfort that lasts for but one day.
I'm desperate for a comfort,
That will come to my life to stay.

How selfishly my heart tries to lead me,
Down pathways that cause me so much pain.
Continue to expose my life,
Until only your presence will remain.

Jesus, I want the comfort you offer.
My needs and desires to you I give.
To your sovereign plan I surrender.
Make me willing your lifestyle to live.

O Lord, I want revival.
Be patient and long-suffering with my ways.
I long to give you more of myself.
I pray that your brokenness will stay.

THE MAKING OF
A WARRIOR

MONTH TWO

The Challenge of Discipleship

Welcome to your second month of "discipleship." I hope and pray that you are becoming consistent with your study time. As you worked through last month, I am sure you had good and bad days. Some days you probably felt like you really got a lot out of your study and enjoyed it. Then there were probably other days that you hated having to study. Just remember that God only asks you to be faithful to study and He has promised to be faithful to speak to you and to teach you. All really great efforts have times of difficulty. If it were easy, everyone would be doing it. Think of it as climbing a mountain. Sometimes the sun is shining and the climb is easy. On other days, you will climb the steepest terrain through blinding rain, sleet or fog. You may not make as much ground but just keep on moving. You have not failed until you quit!

Continue with your Proverbs study. Each month you will be surprised how the Lord will use a different verse to speak to you. If you are struggling with the memory work, now would be the time to get an accountability partner. This person would be someone who could help you memorize your verses. Put your memory verses where you see them each day. They are such an important part of your work.

May the Lord inspire you this month. May He provide the time you need to seek Him. May your desire to know Him increase with each passing day.

This month we will be studying the book of Mark. More commonly referred to as John Mark, he was the cousin of Barnabas and the son of Mary. He helped Paul and Barnabas on their first missionary journey. A problem arose and Paul and Barnabas separated. Barnabas chose to give Mark another chance and in later years, Mark became one of Paul's associates and it all ended well.

The book of Mark details Christ's ministry through Mark's eyes. Mark focused more on Jesus' actions than His words. I can't imagine what it would have been like to sit at the feet of Jesus and hear His stories, can you? I can only imagine how alive the stories must have been to the people who listened. I do know that each individual only received as much as their hearts had the capacity to hear and be changed.

As you begin this month's study, may the Lord open your heart to hear and to be changed. Please pray with me as we begin.

Dear Lord Jesus,

I thank You that knowing You is changing the direction of my life. Thank You that not only have You called me to be your child but You have an ordained purpose for my specific life. I pray that as I study this month that You would increase my capacity to know and understand Your ways as You teach them to me through the Word. May I be so aware of You in my everyday life that I can no longer tell where You begin and where I end. I love You and I ask for more grace to honor and obey Your every desire. In Jesus name.

Sabrina Louise Miller

The Challenge of Discipleship
Month Two - Week One

Week One Checklist

To keep track of how consistent you are becoming in your walk as a disciple, check off your work on this chart as you go. You will either be encouraged as you see your progress or challenged as you see your inconsistency. I am praying that you will be the *"workman that needeth not be ashamed."*

	Bible Study	Memory	Proverbs	Prayer
Sunday				
Monday				
Tuesday				
Wednesday				
Thursday				
Friday				
Saturday				

Prayer Requests

_____

_____

_____

_____

_____

_____

Memory Verses
Month Two - Week One

1 Peter 2:21   *"For even hereunto were ye called: because Christ also suffered for us, leaving us an example, that ye should follow his steps."*

1 Corinthians 4:16   *"Wherefore I beseech you, be ye followers of Me."*

PROVERBS JOURNAL

Proverbs Chapter _____   _____

_____

Proverbs Chapter _____   _____

_____

Proverbs Chapter _____   _____

_____

Proverbs Chapter _____   _____

_____

Proverbs Chapter _____   _____

_____

Proverbs Chapter _____   _____

_____

Proverbs Chapter _____   _____

_____

The Challenge of Discipleship
Month Two - Week One

Day One

The Message of the Cross. . .

As a disciple, what should the cross do for you? There are many kinds of religions and many self-proclaimed gods. For example, today there are 6-7 million Muslims in America. When a friend and I were in New York recently, we had the opportunity to witness to several types of believers. From Catholicism to Hinduism, these people were set in what they believed. It was so sad to not be able to persuade them that Jesus not only died for them, but is now alive and sitting at the right hand of the Father, making intercession for them. All their gods are dead gods. Our God, the one true God, is alive. Christianity is the only faith where the one served and honored was willing to give up His life that we might have eternal life. Have you ever really seen the reality of the cross in your life? Discipleship means that we are willing to die to our rights and all our selfish dreams. It may seem like you have to die to everything…and you do. But I can promise you, Jesus will not fail you.

I have been through a lot in my own personal life. The loss and abandonment of both my parents, I was sexually and physically abused as a child, and I have been rejected by siblings for the cause of Christ. I also have a stained and scarred past from my own willful sin. Yet, all is well. Jesus is a friend like no other. When everyone else forsakes me, He never does.

So many of you are hungry to know Him in an intimate way. Let Jesus take you to the cross and lay your burdens there. Don't carry any burdens with you, I don't care how bad your sin is. Give it up. Give it to Him and watch Him deliver you. He is faithful.

Begin this week by memorizing your two verses for the week.

1 Peter 2:21   *"For even hereunto were ye called: because Christ also suffered for us, leaving us an example, that ye should follow his steps."*

1 Corinthians 4:16   *"Wherefore I beseech you, be ye followers of Me."*

What kind of a follower are you? Do you follow in His steps? Let's begin our study with Mark, Chapter 1, the second book in the New Testament. Read the chapter and answer the following questions:

1. John the Baptist was really different. Tell me a few things about him. How did he dress? What did he eat?

2. Each one of us was born for a God-ordained purpose. What was John the Baptist's purpose in life?

3. When John baptized Jesus, what did the Father say?

4. Have you been baptized? Being baptized may seem like a meaningless ritual to you, but it is very important. Jesus role-modeled it to us in John. If you have not been baptized, you need to talk to your pastor or Sunday School leader about the importance of this act of obedience.

5. List the names of the disciples that Jesus calls in this chapter.

6. List the three miracles that take place in chapter one.

    a)

    b)

    c)

Read the proverb of the day and write in your journal.

Day Two

Let's begin our lesson by looking at the call of discipleship. Did you know each one of us was created with a God-vacuum inside us? The vacuum can only be satisfied by filling it with purpose, His purpose. That purpose is our God-ordained call to follow Him in discipleship. Notice I said it could only be satisfied by God. You may try to fill it with other things, but you can never satisfy it.

THY WORD IS A
LAMP UNTO MY FEET
AND A LIGHT UNTO
MY PATH…

Read Mark, Chapter 2 and answer the following questions:

1. As Jesus' ministry continued, there were so many people pleading with Him to be healed. Why did Jesus heal the man who was sick of the palsy?

2. What were the scribes reaction to this miracle?

3. Which disciple did He call in chapter 2?

4. What type of people did Jesus say He came to minister to?

5. What was Jesus trying to say in verses 23-27?

The bottom line is that the Lord heals when it pleases Him. In the healing of the paralytic, we are overwhelmed with the compassion of Christ, as we should be. But, He doesn't always heal. Many times He uses sickness to get our attention or to glorify Himself. Remember, He is glorified in our weaknesses.

If you know Him as your personal Saviour, you have witnessed a miracle. Please realize that when He forgave your sins, He performed an eternal miracle. As you continue to follow Him, don't lose your "awe" over what He has done and what He is doing. The fact that you want to surrender your life to Him is a miracle in itself, isn't it?

With all these miracles you've been studying, you may be wondering why so many are sick among us. There are actually three kinds of sickness; there is a sickness unto chastisement, a sickness unto the glory of God, and a sickness unto death. Let's look at each one.

First, write out James 5:15.

_____

_____

_____

_____

1. The first sickness is called a sickness unto chastisement. Sometimes, when we practice habitual sin, the Lord has to allow affliction to gain our attention.

2. Sometimes the sicknes in one's life is simply placed there to bring glory to the Lord. We call that a sickness unto the glory of God. Write out John 9:1-3.

_____

_____

_____

_____

3. Finally, there is a sickness unto death. There is a place of disobedience in the believer's life where they willfully choose sin over and over again no matter how much the Lord deals with them. The Lord can then choose to bring the believer home to preserve His name. This sickness can be found in 1 John 5:16.

In all three examples of sickness, the Lord has a purpose to accomplish. If you are suffering with physical sickness, you should ask the Lord for direction in what He is trying to show you. His wisdom can be found. Be sure to seek Him with your whole heart. Don't ever be afraid to cry out for healing. He heals a broken heart and He can heal a broken body.

May He bless your day with wisdom from on high.

Read the proverb of the day and write in your journal.

Day Three

Start today by writing out your memory verses and then read your poem:

1 Peter 2:21

_____

_____

Corinthians 4:16

_____

_____

Read Mark, Chapter 3 and answer the following questions:

1. What was the miracle performed in the first five verses?

2. What is the one sin that can never be forgiven?

3. Who did Jesus say were His mother, His brothers and sister?

   Let's review verses 28-30. Although Jesus will forgive men of all their sins, He cannot forgive denying the Holy Spirit as these men were doing. They were contributing the power of God to a demon. Do we really realize the power and the supremacy of who the Holy Spirit is in our lives today? What would it be like without His voice to direct our path, correct us or warn us of the dangers to come? Thank Him as you pray today for being with you. It is a precious gift to hear the voice of God through the Holy Spirit.

Read the proverb of the day and write in your journal.

WILL YOU FOLLOW?

Jesus asked His disciples this simple question,
"Will you follow Me?"
Somewhere in your lifetime,
These same words can set you free.

Following Jesus will bring you freedom,
From yourself and from your sin.
But you have noticed few will follow,
For there's a battle you must win.

Some days following will be easy,
And the price to pay will not be high.
But other days will seem to cost you everything,
And to all your dreams you'll have to die.

On those days you must cry out to Him,
And let His favor become your prize.
Just to know that you have pleased Him,
Will overcome the doubt that's sure to arise.

Follow Jesus friend, let me encourage you,
To His voice and call stay true.
When the end of this process is over,
Your life will be made brand new.

Day Four

While we continue to think on "discipleship," I hope you are beginning to see that the Savior we follow asks a lot. Yet He supplies even more than imaginable. So far, we have read about several miracles. These were hopeless situations where His simple command changed the lives of those people forever.

Maybe you have given up on a situation in your life. It just seems so hopeless. Maybe it's doing this study. Maybe it just doesn't matter to you or seems dull and boring. I know that I have not always enjoyed reading the Word. I am not some kind of unique individual who was born motivated to read the Bible. The Lord has given me the desire to read it and that means He can do the same for you if you will ask Him.

Blind? Ask. Bored? Ask. Hopeless? Ask. What is the situation(s) in your life that seem(s) hopeless today? What situation do you find yourself powerless in? Any place where there is no hope and no answer is the exact location where Jesus will show up. That's the kind of Savior He is.

Write out a prayer acknowledging Jesus as a miracle-working God. Then tell Him about your need.

Dear Jesus,

Read Mark, Chapter 4 and answer the following questions:

1. List the four kinds of ground.

    a)   b)

    c)   d)

2. What happened to the seed sown on the wayside?

3. Why was the seed scorched that was planted on stony ground?

4. What happened to the seed sown among the thorns?

5. What yield did the seed gain on good ground?

6. In verses 14-20, the seed falls on four types of ground, let's look at each one.

    *   The wayside heart was a heart of no commitment. This heart heard the Word but was divided against itself. With no commitment, there is no root.

    *   The stony heart is a shallow heart. It hears the Word but doesn't apply it, so there is no change.

    *   The thorny heart is the saddest heart of all. No matter what part of the Word it hears, it allows the cares of this world and the deceitfulness of riches to choke it out.

    *   The good ground is a Kingdom heart. This is a thirsty and seeking heart. This heart hears the Word and applies it.

7. What kind of heart do you have?

8. What miracle did Jesus use in verses 35-41 to expose their lack of faith?

Read the proverb of the day and write in your journal.

Day Five

What would cause twelve men to give up everything in their lives? What would cause them to leave their jobs, their homes, to forsake all to be a disciple? I tell you, my friend, when we see Jesus like they saw Jesus, we would be willing to lay it all down as well. I encourage you, as you study these stories, to let the Lord show you who He is. If you suffer with a lack of interest concerning the things of the Lord, you probably have never seen Him. Ask Him to meet with you as you study.

Begin today by reading Mark 5 and answering the following questions:

1. In the story of the Gadarean demon-possessed man, how many demons were there?

   Where did Jesus send them?

2. What did Jesus tell the man to do after he was healed?

3. List the other three miracles in Mark 5.

   a)

   b)

   c)

A miracle is an earthly event with a heavenly explanation. If you have been saved, then you have experienced a miracle. Do you know anyone who has experienced a miracle in their life? Miracles awaken us to the kingdom of God. It takes a real commitment on our part to walk with miracle-faith in the everyday, mundane things of life.

If we could embrace our everyday lives with a kingdom purpose, each day could become an adventure to us. What will the Lord show us today? What person will He bring into our path to share with, to minister to? When all our days become days lived for Him, then we can see life though His eyes. The disciples were willing to give up everything to follow Christ. Please don't misunderstand me, following Jesus is not a list of do's and don'ts. Following Jesus should be the desire of your life. To deny yourself means that you are so in love with Jesus that you are willing to serve Him by giving up all rights to yourself. When you become a disciple of Jesus, you surrender your rights, you give up your own life and your own way. If your life is filled with things you won't need in your desire to have an intimate life with Christ, my prayer is that you will allow the Lord to guide you in what you need to remove in your life to stay effective in the kingdom.

OPEN OUR EYES

Open our eyes, Lord, to see your plan,
Following You is our desire.
Teach us from Your Word and let us see,
What discipleship will require.

We don't want to be ordinary people,
May the world see a difference - we pray.
In order to fulfill our destiny, Lord,
We are willing to die each day to our way.

The world offers many options to us,
From sports to popularity and fame.
But we have seen your face and believe,
That happiness is found in pursuit of your name.

You have called us to Kindom living,
Many dreams and plans for us You have shown.
We'll study Your Word and apply ourselves,
Lving daily to make your message known.

Read the proverb of the day and write in your journal.

Day Six

Read Mark, Chapter 6 and answer the following questions:

1. In verses 1-6, Mark explains why Jesus could not do miracles in His own hometown. Why was that?

2. In verse 7, Jesus sent out the twelve. List at least three things He told them to do.

   a)

   b)

   c)

3. In verses 12 and 13, how effective was the disciples' early ministry?

4. Who did Herod believe Jesus was?

5. How had Herod killed John the Baptist?

6. Why did Jesus have compassion toward the people? (v. 34)

7. When Jesus asked how many loaves there were, how did the disciples reply?

8. How much bread was left over?

Just as Jesus sent out His disciples in this chapter, if you are His disciple, you have been sent out also. As you live out each day, do you see yourself as His "ambassador?"

Webster defines an ambassador as, *"an authorized messenger."* You have been given authority and a message. Are you fulfilling that role in your life today?

9. How many did they feed?

10. In verse 52, why did they not consider the miracle of the loaves?

In the feeding of the 5,000, Jesus was teaching His disciples to have compassion for the hungry. He fed them by performing a miracle. In our world, there are so many spiritually hungry people. The Lord would desire that you have His heart for those He places in your life. Teaching them to feed on God's Word and on His promises will insure them against ever being hungry again. Do you have a friend that is physically hungry? Buy him dinner but while you're there, share Jesus with him and you will be practicing discipleship.

Let me ask you a question. Is there an area in your life where you can testify that God performed a miracle? How long has it been since you thought about that time? When was the last time you shared about it with someone? The disciples quickly forgot the feeding of the 5,000 and their hearts were hardened. That means they had unbelief. Boy, do I relate. How soon I forget all He has done for me. When I do forget, I fail to believe for the trials I am presently going through. Today, thank Him for all the miracles He has performed in your life. Especially, may we be grateful for His presence in our lives.

As we continue to study the life of Jesus and the miracles He performed, I want to encourage you to seek to know Him more. Also, cry out to Him with your needs. God has been so faithful to me this past year. Time and time again I have seen miracles in my own life, big and small. I want you to know Him like that. Say your memory verses to someone today.

Dear Lord,

I feel You calling me, to trust You for my every need. You alone could feed the hungry. Touching their lives and filling up their empty places. I lay my life before You today. Crying out for Your mercy to be displayed through me. I am hungry, so hungry—feed me, Lord, I pray. In Jesus name, Amen.

Read the proverb of the day and write in your journal.

Day Seven

Overcoming our selfish desires each day is the only way we can stay in process. Sometimes, however, we simply lose our desire to fight. Maybe we've been hurt by someone or have disappointed someone dear to us. You wake up and think, "It's just not worth it." At that point of weakness, the enemy will swoop in on you. Don't listen to the voices. They'll only lead you away from the path of righteousness. Once you start listening to them, they will begin to weaken your resolve to trust the Lord. The Lord allows tests and trials in your life for a purpose. He wants to show you that you are capable of more than you realize. Remember, faith is one step beyond what you can accomplish on your own. Whatever your battle has been this week, trust the Lord. He alone is able to deliver you. Persevere in your study. Everyday you are being transformed into the man or woman of God He has planned. You will overcome, just keep trying.

OVERCOMING

To us it has been given the grace to overcome.
Yet we know we can't without power from above.

As we cry out to You, our sins are daily exposed.
You free us from the strongholds and victory becomes ours to hold.

Overcoming is a process, but to Your Word You stay true.
We may make mistakes, but consistency is there when the process is through.

To some it may seem too simple to just cry "I can't" - Lord come.
He loves my childlike cry as I choose against the darkness I am from.

I am walking daily beside a King, of course there are lessons to learn.
But falling or slipping a bit is not an excuse to run.

I am being prepared for His purposes, everyday new ground I take.
I trust Him for the end result, overcoming no matter my mistakes.

Read the proverb of the day and write in your journal.

The Challenge of Discipleship
Month Two - Week Two

Week Two Checklist

To keep track of how consistent you are becoming in your walk as a disciple, check off your work on this chart as you go. You will either be encouraged as you see your progress or challenged as you see your inconsistency. I am praying that you will be the *"workman that needeth not be ashamed."*

	Bible Study	Memory	Proverbs	Prayer
Sunday	_____	_____	_____	_____
Monday	_____	_____	_____	_____
Tuesday	_____	_____	_____	_____
Wednesday	_____	_____	_____	_____
Thursday	_____	_____	_____	_____
Friday	_____	_____	_____	_____
Saturday	_____	_____	_____	_____

Prayer Requests

_____

_____

_____

_____

_____

_____

Memory Verses
Month Two - Week Two

1 Cor. 6:19
*"What? know ye not that your body is the temple of the Holy Ghost
which is in you, which ye have of God, and ye are not your own?"*

1 Cor. 6:20
*"For ye are bought with a price: therefore glorify God
in your body, and in your spirit, which are God's."*

PROVERBS JOURNAL

Proverbs Chapter _____ _____

_____

Proverbs Chapter _____ _____

_____

Proverbs Chapter _____ _____

_____

Proverbs Chapter _____ _____

_____

Proverbs Chapter _____ _____

_____

Proverbs Chapter _____ _____

_____

Proverbs Chapter _____ _____

_____

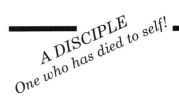

The Challenge of Discipleship
Month Two - Week Two

Day One

One of the ways you can tell a disciple apart from a believer is the absence of rights. When Jesus called the disciples, they gave up all their rights. The absence of rights... now that's a high call. It seems like we are easily offended, wouldn't you agree? Yet, as the disciples followed Jesus, they didn't get the opportunity to be angry or resentful. They were like dead people who had been resurrected with a purpose, a mission or cause. Their desire was to please the Lord. They sought to have a heart like His. Is there any place in the Word you can find the Lord whining or complaining because He had His feelings hurt? I don't think so. He had come to earth to fulfill a life mission, a call. What about you? Can you trust the Lord to show you His purpose for your life—everyday— the rest of your life? Remember, surrendering your rights gives Him the right to be glorified. Let's take a look at this week's verses.

> **1 Corinthians 6:19** *"What? Know ye not that your body is the temple of the Holy Ghost which is in you, which ye have of God, and ye are not your own?"*

> **1 Corinthians 6:20** *"For ye are bought with a price; therefore glorify God in your body and in your spirit which is God's."*

Read Mark, Chapter 7 and answer the following questions:

1. What was the complaint of the Pharisees in the opening part of the chapter?

2. Much of the time, we clean up the outside and ignore the inside. In verse 6, Jesus identifies the problem—their hearts are far from Him. What about you? Do you feel as clean on the inside as you look on the outside?

3. What does verse 15 mean to you?

4. What was the miracle in this chapter?

5. In the healing of the deaf man, Jesus does a very unusual thing. What was it?

6. Do you think that the healing was found in His spit or was it in His obedience to do what the Father was instructing Him to do?

As you begin to memorize these verses, let's take a closer look at them. Sometimes, when you get saved, you don't realize that you are giving up your rights to yourself. Maybe you understood that you were in need of salvation and even saw yourself as a sinner. Did you realize how much the presence of Jesus in your life would affect your everyday life? These two verses sum up the call of "discipleship" or the call of "dying to your rights." When you were saved, you surrendered your mind as well as your body to Jesus and what He wants. Following Him can be very simple. Just ask yourself how Jesus would act in this situation. Then respond like He would. You may be asking, "How do I know what to do?" That's where studying the gospels is so exciting. In Matthew, Mark, Luke and John, we read everyday stories of the Lord Jesus as He walked the earth.

Let's begin our new week by asking the Lord to make His Word alive to you. Many mornings I've begun my study time by acknowledging to the Lord that I am ashamed of how slow my progress has been. I fall short so many times, but each time I pick up my Bible and start reading. Without fail, His Word speaks to me. Words of encouragement and hope. *"He never said I could, but He always said He would."* Don't quit. Don't give up. Don't allow the study of His Word to become routine. Expect Him to say something to you, maybe something you have never read or heard before. Write out a prayer for this week's quiet time.

Dear Jesus,

Please use my quiet time this week to...

_____

_____

_____

_____

_____

Read the proverb of the day and write in your journal.

Day Two

Have you ever stopped to wonder why there are so few people who follow Christ? Let's face it. Most of the world is extremely busy enjoying all the world has to offer. So why would it be any different with you? Even now, the enemy is busy devising a plan to distract you from God's purpose for your life.

Well, I believe the difference is found in today's passage. When Jesus asks Peter the question, *"Who do you say that I am?"* He was confronting Peter with a personal salvation. Following Jesus, as you see Him in your everyday life, will produce the heart of a disciple. The heart of one who is not easily distracted from his life-calling.

Each individual person has a unique calling and purpose for being alive in this world today. What about you? Do you realize your purpose?

Who do you say Jesus is? Is He your Lord? Does He have the right to take you and spend you on His purpose?

As you study today, expect the Lord to be as personal with you as He was with Peter. Can you say with Peter, *"You are the Christ"*?

Before you read Mark, Chapter 8, see if you can write out Mark 8:34 and 35 from memory. (They were some of your memory verses from last month.) I have written the first couple of words for you.

Mark 8:34b *"Whosoever will* _____

_____

_____

_____

Mark 8:35 *"For whosoever will* _____

_____

_____

_____

_____

_____

_____

Now read Mark 8 and answer the following questions:

1. Why did Jesus feed the multitude? (v.2-3)

2. How many loaves did the disciples have?

3. What did Jesus do with those loaves?

4. How many were fed that day?

5. How many baskets were left over when He fed the 5,000?

6. How many were left over when He fed the 4,000?

7. Where did Jesus deal with a blind man?

8. What was Peter's response when Jesus asked him, *"Whom do men say that I am?"*

9. Now let me ask you, who do you say He is?

10. In verse 38, Jesus warns that when He returns, He will be ashamed of us if we what?

Read the proverb of the day and write in your journal.

Day Three

The road to holiness, that's the road of the disciple. It leads us straight to the cross and through the cross we are set free. Before Christ went to the cross, we were slaves to the enemy. He owned us. He had the rights to us. The cross is an instrument of deliverance. An instrument is a means by which something is done. Isaiah 61:1 says, *"The Spirit of the Lord God is upon me; because the Lord hath anointed me to preach good tidings unto the meek; he hath sent me to bind up the brokenhearted, to proclaim liberty to the captives, and the opening of the prison to them that are bound."*

Satan cannot keep you out of heaven if you have been predestined to the cross. He cannot stop it from happening. Satan can keep you bound in sin, defeated and discouraged. However, you may be saved, but you'll have no impact on the Kingdom of God. The cross is your instrument of deliverance. Go to the cross of Calvary and find your deliverance. Claim it. In your life today, is there any area that you can't control? Cry out to Jesus. His death at the cross makes possible your deliverance. If you are battling sin today, pray Psalms 34 over your life. Fight, O mighty warrior, fight!

Read Mark 9 and answer the following questions:

1. What Peter, James, and John experienced on the mountaintop must have been amazing to them. What an honor to have been chosen to go with Him. As He was transfigured before their eyes, what do you think they must have felt?

2. What would you have felt?

3. As you read the miracle in John 9, what did you learn?

4. How did Jesus teach the disciples that they could become first?

5. What is one way you could live that out in your life today?

6. What did Jesus say about the little children?

7. How do you see little children?

8. Are you looking for opportunities to minister to children?

9. A man brought his demonized child to Jesus. What did Jesus say was possible if he believed?

10. What was the man's response in verse 24?

Is there any area where you have unbelief? Any area you can't overcome? Maybe you feel as trapped by the enemy as this boy did. Unbelief ties you to your sin. Maybe it has confused you and you think you can't live without it. That's a lie.

Let's take a closer look at our memory verses this week. God has called us to a walk of holiness. He purchased the right to control our minds and our bodies with His death on Calvary. In Mark, Chapter 9, you just read that if your arm or your eye offends you, it would be better to cut if off than to be disobedient to the Lord. What would you say is the greatest area of struggle in your life in glorifying Jesus in your body? Take the last week of your life, where would you not have wanted Jesus to go with you? Did you use your body, in any way, to watch or think or take part in something that didn't glorify God? Today would be a great day to confess and forsake that, thereby cutting it off from your life. Never be discouraged with your failures. Remember, you have not failed until you quit.

- DON'T QUIT -

Let's pray together.

Dear Lord Jesus,

There are areas in my life that I am now aware of that I need to remove. I ask You today to forgive me for my willful choice to add these things to my life. As You forgive me, I pray that You would remove _____ from my life and cleanse me from every desire connected to these sins. Lord, I want to exemplify Your character in my everyday living. Knowing You and loving You is the most rewarding thing in my life. Today I am surrendering these areas to You that Your light might shine through me. Thank You for loving me in spite of my stupid moments and thank You for changing me. I love You. In Jesus name.

Read the proverb of the day and write in your journal.

Day Four

Today we'll study about the rich, young ruler. You may be thinking, *"How does this apply to me? I have about twenty dollars in the bank."* Well, the Lord wasn't just dealing with this young man's pocketbook. He was dealing with his heart. Now, ask yourself again, *"How does this apply to me?"* What do I need more than Jesus?

Read Mark, Chapter 10 and answer the following questions:

1. The world has an opinion on divorce and your friends have an opinion on divorce. What did Jesus say about divorce?

2. Jesus received the children. They were of great value to Him. In verse 15, what did Jesus say?

3. Jesus wants us to be as trusting as a little child is of his parents. Do you trust Him like that?

4. What was the rich, young ruler's posture as he came to Jesus?

5. Was he sincere in his quest to find eternal life?

6. Had he kept the commandments that Jesus required?

7. How did Jesus feel toward the young man?

8. What was the rich, young ruler's response to what Jesus required of him?

9. When Peter mentions to Jesus that he has left all to follow Him, what is Jesus' response? (Notice that He promises Peter these things in his lifetime.)

10. As you read verses 35-40, notice that Jesus is teaching on the sovereignty of God. Sovereignty is us recognizing that before the foundation of the world, Jesus had decided how our lives would be lived out. Sovereignty is God being absolutely in control of everything—everyday. The exciting thing is He created us with a free will. So, even though He knows what our choices will be, He allows us to make them. How did Jesus say we could become the greatest in the kingdom of God?

ONLY JESUS REALLY KNOWS YOUR HEART

The rich young ruler came to Jesus,
A need in his life to fill.
Having religiously kept all the commandments,
Still looking for a relationship that was real.

Jesus only asked one thing of him,
A difficult task you'd agree.
But knowing covetousness held his heart,
Salvation alone would set him free.

Each day we come to Jesus.
He alone can bring real change.
When we fall, He'll pick us up,
And our Kingdom mistakes rearrange.

'Til we've quit - we have not failed,
Faithfully He'll finish the work He starts.
He'll remove the obstacles in our path,
If we'll follow Him with a pure heart.

Read the proverb of the day and write in your journal.

Day Five

The cross is an instrument of deliverance. Yet, the work of the cross is not a one time decision. You must decide to make your way back to the cross, everyday of your life. It is a daily decision. Your flesh will fight you, the world will fight you, and the devil will fight you. If you will allow the work of the cross, thus death to yourself, to be a daily decision, you will become the overcomer the Lord has called you to be.

Through your trials you come to know the Lord and learn to trust Him. What is one thing you know you never could have done if the Lord hadn't helped you? Today, look for an opportunity to share that victory with someone. Give the Lord the glory due unto His name.

Read Mark, Chapter 11 and answer the following questions:

1. What type of entry did Jesus make going into Jerusalem?

2. Why did Jesus curse the fig tree?

3. What point do you think He was trying to make?

4. Jesus really knew how to clean the temple out, didn't He? Can't you just see Him throwing people out and overturning tables? We just don't think of Him as being that confrontational. What did He want His house to be called?

5. Notice that just after teaching us how to remove a mountain by our faith, the Lord teaches on forgiveness. As we studied last month, we cannot operate in faith as a disciple if we do not walk in forgiveness toward our fellow man. What are the consequences of unforgiveness?

Forgiveness is not:

Forgiveness is not saying that what happened to you was good!

Forgiveness is not saying that you have to spend time with those who have wounded you!

Forgiveness is not saying that you weren't hurt by what happened!

Forgiveness is not saying you can do that again!

Forgiveness is not saying that there are no consequences to what happened!

Forgiveness is:

Forgiveness is you realizing you've been wronged, but being willing to "release" your offender!

Forgiveness is you releasing yourself from those who hurt you!

Forgiveness is believing that others deserve your forgiveness because Jesus has forgiven you!

Forgiveness ultimately frees us from those who have wounded us. It gives us the opportunity to take something bad and see the Lord do something good with it.

Forgiveness requires death on your part. You don't get to pay back or hold a grudge. It gives you the opportunity to be like Jesus. I know it's a high call. Few follow here. I am praying you'll be one of the few.

Read the proverb of the day and write in your journal.

Day Six

While you thought about giving up your rights this week, did you think about the benefits of allowing the Lord to have control? He has promised to never leave you or forsake you. He has promised to meet your every need. He is a friend like no other.

Read Mark, Chapter 12 and answer the following questions:

1. What did Jesus have to say about paying taxes?

2. When asked if we would be married in heaven, what was Jesus' response? How do you feel about this?

Remember, no one on earth really has a clue about heaven. No one can say, *"Been there, done that."* His Word does tell us of heaven's beauty and how wonderful it is. However, God must like surprises because He has left out a lot of details for us to ponder. We should just trust Him with marriage and all the other things we don't understand about heaven.

HEAVEN…DON'T MISS IT FOR THE WORLD!

Maybe you feel that heaven will be a disappointment after your life here on planet earth. Ask the Lord to give you a vision, a hope of all heaven will be. I imagine heaven to be breathtaking and beyond my wildest dreams. To serve Jesus eternally, without reservation, just imagine! We will be living in His love and total acceptance without human restraints.

3. What did Jesus teach was the first commandment?

Loving the Lord with all your heart is a commandment. Loving the Lord should come out of a heart of gratefulness for all He has done. Do you love Him with all your heart? Tell Him so on the following page.

Dear Jesus,

_____

_____

_____

_____

_____

_____

_____

_____

_____

_____

_____

4. What was the second commandment?

5. Jesus wants you to treat your neighbor with love and understanding. Here He says you are to treat them as you would yourself. Do you treat yourself fairly or are you demanding and unforgiving toward yourself?

6. Why was Jesus so impressed with the widow's offering?

7. How about you? How do you give? Out of your abundance or out of your need?

Read the proverb of the day and write in your journal.

Day Seven

Reading God's Word, spending time with Him in prayer—I don't know about you, but I see how far I still have to go. I am so thankful that His mercies are new each morning.

The Word talks about Jesus being the very breath I breathe. That is my prayer and I hope it is your prayer also. No matter how much Jesus is showing you what needs to be killed in your life, just don't give up. Run to Him and let the river of His love encourage and refresh you as it cleanses. I pray that His Word will point you to Him and to His deep abiding love for you. Remember, He has promised to return for us. Heaven is going to be a wonderful surprise to all of us. Then we will understand how valuable our relationship with Him truly is.

Read Mark, Chapter 13 and list at least eight signs of the coming of the Lord.

1.

2.

3.

4.

5.

6.

7.

8.

WHO DO YOU SAY THAT JESUS IS?

Jesus asks, "Whom do men say that I am?"
He asks us to profess the answer in how we live.
Being a disciple is to follow His life,
Being willing to give up anything He asks you to give.

Whom do you say that Jesus is?
Does your life live out what you believe?
Is He Lord and Master in all you do?
Have you His call on your life received?

Don't make it harder than it is.
To follow Him is worth it all.
He'll meet your needs and direct your path.
A friend who will come when you call.

Others may have let you down,
Following them has brought you pain.
But, my friend, if you follow Jesus I can promise.
Contentment will be your gain.

Read the proverb of the day and write in your journal.

The Challenge of Discipleship
Month Two - Week Three

Week Three Checklist

To keep track of how consistent you are becoming in your walk as a disciple, check off your work on this chart as you go. You will either be encouraged as you see your progress or challenged as you see your inconsistency. I am praying that you will be the *"workman that needeth not be ashamed."*

	Bible Study	Memory	Proverbs	Prayer
Sunday	_____	_____	_____	_____
Monday	_____	_____	_____	_____
Tuesday	_____	_____	_____	_____
Wednesday	_____	_____	_____	_____
Thursday	_____	_____	_____	_____
Friday	_____	_____	_____	_____
Saturday	_____	_____	_____	_____

Prayer Requests

_____

_____

_____

_____

_____

Memory Verses
Month Two - Week Three

Romans 6:1
"What shall we say then? Shall we continue in sin, that grace may abound?"

Romans 6:2
"God forbid. How shall we, that are dead to sin, live any longer therein?"

PROVERBS JOURNAL

Proverbs Chapter _____ _____

_____

Proverbs Chapter _____ _____

_____

Proverbs Chapter _____ _____

_____

Proverbs Chapter _____ _____

_____

Proverbs Chapter _____ _____

_____

Proverbs Chapter _____ _____

_____

Proverbs Chapter _____ _____

_____

A DISCIPLE
One who is willing to endure!

The Challenge of Discipleship
Month Two - Week Three

Day One

Welcome to another week of Bible study. Have you ever wondered why so many people go away after having followed the Lord for awhile? I have found that there are many reasons people quit.

*   It's simply too hard. They are not willing to discipline their lives.

*   At times, following the Lord can be very lonely. If you don't learn to fellowship with Him, you'll quit.

*   Many people quit because of willful sin. They are slaves to sin and as slaves, they choose to remain.

As a disciple, you must be willing to endure; endure boredom, persecution, failure and success. I am praying for you that you will not grow weary. The following are your memory verses for the third week.

Romans 6:1   *"What shall we say then? Shall we continue to live in sin, that grace may abound?"*

Romans 6:2   *"God forbid. How shall we, that are dead to sin, live any longer therein?"*

Read Mark, Chapter 14 and answer the following questions:

1. Why did the people get upset with the woman who anointed Jesus' feet?

2. The disciples took the very first communion with Jesus. They partook looking toward the cross and we partake looking back to the cross. What did the bread represent? What did the cup represent?

3. Has there been a time in your life when you denied Christ?

4. At Gethsemane, the disciples experienced what you experience in trying to do your quiet time. They wanted to stay awake, they meant to stay awake, but they didn't. All their good intentions fell by the wayside. When Jesus found them sleeping, what did He say?

5. Who led the group that came to arrest Jesus?

6. When asked if he was Jesus, the Christ, how did Jesus respond?

7. List the three times that Peter denied Christ.

   a)

   b)

   c)

The story of Peter's denial is one of my favorite passages in the Bible. That's because I have also denied Christ. I have denied Him in my attitudes, in my actions, and I have felt the shame and humiliation that Peter must have felt. I love how the Lord knew I would need to read of another who failed, just like I have. Don't you love the Word of God? Doesn't it give you great hope to know that Peter, the one who denied Christ, was the disciple who was chosen to be the rock to build the church upon? Maybe there is hope for you and I!

Thank you for studying today. May the Word of God bless you and encourage you.

Read the proverb of the day and write in your journal.

Day Two

As I continue to study the call of "discipleship" in my own personal life, I am amazed at how far I miss the mark. How are you doing? Are you finding consistency in your life? Please remember that when we do fail, it pleases the Lord for us to try again. He covers us so that we might begin again. His ultimate plan for us is to overcome no matter how many times we fail. Can you hear Him? Don't quit. Don't quit. See Jesus today as you read your chapter in Mark. See what an overcoming life He walked upon this earth. Determine that no matter how many times you falter, you will daily choose to follow in His steps.

Read Mark, Chapter 15 and answer the following questions:

1. Pilate offered to release a particular prisoner because of the feast they were celebrating. Which prisoner did they choose to release?

2. Do you think they realized they were just pawns in the Father's hands?_____
   No matter what is going on in the world that you do not understand, know the Father is working all things for our good. He is in control of all things. The Father planned and ordained the crucifixion of His son. None of it caught Him by surprise. Read the rest of this chapter in Mark and think about what it might have felt like to be Jesus.

3. Was the release of Barrabas a mistake or was it the will of God?

4. What do you think Jesus thought as He endured each level of suffering involved in this chapter? Write your thoughts below and explain.

   I think Jesus may have had these thoughts as He walked through the "process" of His crucifixion:

   _____

   _____

   _____

   _____

   _____

There is no human way we can fully understand all the Lord endured during His crucifixion. His separation from His heavenly Father was the most difficult part of all. Jesus knew He had been born to die, but He was still human in His emotions. When you are lonely, when you are afraid, try to remember all Jesus endured and seek Him. I want to encourage you to be consistent in your pursuit of Him. He will never fail you, I promise.

HE DIED THAT WE MIGHT LIVE

Jesus saved me that I might live,
His death provided the way.
Though trials and temptations continue to come,
On the road of "discipleship" I choose to stay.

Let my life be different, Lord,
Than it was before you came.
May your voice direct my paths,
Keeping me from all shame.

Jesus, knowing you is my desire,
Though at times I may not understand.
I'm trusting daily in Your word,
Only placing my life in Your hand.

I may be empty and restless at times,
Other voices may call my name.
But like Peter I'll focus on your face,
And to the "disciple" call remain.

Read the proverb of the day and write in your journal.

Day Three

DOES MY SACRIFICE LIVE?
(Oswald Chambers)

"And Abraham built an altar… and bound Isaac, his son." (Genesis 22:9) This incident is a picture of the blunder we make in thinking that the final thing God wants of us is the sacrifice of death. What God wants is the sacrifice <u>through</u> death which enables us to do what Jesus did—sacrifice our lives. It's not "I am willing to go to death with Thee." It's, "I am willing to be identified with Thy death, that I may sacrifice my life to God." We seem to think that God wants us to give up things! God purified Abraham from this blunder and the same discipline goes on in our lives. Nowhere does God tell us to give up things for the sake of giving them up. He tells us to give them up for the sake of the only thing worth having—life with Himself. It is a question of loosening the bands that hinder our lives. Immediately those bands are loosened by identification with the death of Jesus and we enter into a relationship with God whereby we can sacrifice our lives to Him.

It is of no value to God to give Him your life for death. He wants you be a "living sacrifice," to let Him have all your powers that have been saved and sanctified through Jesus. "This is the thing that is acceptable to God."

*Oswald Chambers, January 8th

We have studied the crucifixion and attempted to identify some of the thoughts the Lord might have had as He went through that process. Maybe, as you have studied "discipleship", you feel as if Jesus wants you to be as a dead person. That is so far from the truth.The very reason that He died is that we might live. Following Jesus is the most "alive" thing you can do. He longs to have you live for Him. As you study today, ask yourself, "Am I alive to God or am I just dead to sin?" The world has enough dead, boring Christians. He is looking for a generation of passionate believers who are willing to invest everything in following Him to an abiding, alive life.

Read Mark, Chapter 16 and answer the following questions:

1. What is the main difference in the God we serve as opposed to Muhammad or Allah? If Jesus had just died and been buried, like everyone else in the world, then our faith would be no different than the rest. His story only began in the

tomb. There He won the victory that we might live unto eternal life. Who was the first one to discover that He had been resurrected?

2. To whom did Jesus appear first?

3. When Jesus walked with the two on the road, what was their reaction?

4. When Jesus appeared unto the twelve, what two things did Jesus upbraided them for?

    a)

    b)

5. This was a pretty important meeting. They thought Jesus was dead and now there He stood before them—alive! What did Jesus tell them?

6. What were the signs Jesus said would follow those who believe?

7. Where is Jesus now?

8. What did the disciples do after Jesus left them?

9. Are you a disciple?

10. Are you following Jesus in the way His disciples followed?

Read the proverb of the day and write in your journal.

Day Four

Today, we will begin a study in the book of Romans. Romans is one of my favorite books in the Bible but it does contain some very interesting words. Let me introduce a few of them to you.

Faith - Faith is believing, it is knowing, it is substance, it is being ready to stake your life on what you believe.

Righteousness - Righteousness is right being. It is not just right doing.

Justified - Having my sins erased.

Sanctification - Means to be set apart.

Paul wrote the book of Romans and sent it on to the believers in Rome before he was actually able to be there. It is the single most important doctrinal book in the Bible. When you can understand Romans, you can understand so much more of the Bible. If I were to give this book a title, I would entitle it, *How God Saves A Sinnner*. As you study, ask the Holy Spirit to show you the pictures Paul's introducing to you. See yourself as a sinner first and as a saint second. As you read today, place your name in verse 16.

1. Who wrote the book of Romans?

2. In verse 1, Paul tells three things about himself. What are they?

    a)

    b)

    c)

3. What does he say about us in verse 6?

4. In verse 16, Paul declares that he is not ashamed of the gospel of Christ. What does he declare that the gospel is?

5. Is it like that in your life? Paul had met Jesus on the road to Damascus and his life radically changed. Have you? Do you know Him like Paul does?

6. Romans 1 describes the downward spiral of a man or woman, boy or girl who turn their back on righteousness. Let's trace this spiral. In verse 18, "who" is the wrath of God revealed against?

7. In verse 19, Paul tells us why God is angry with those who hold on to ungodliness and unrighteousness. Why is He angry?

8. In verse 21, when these people knew God, they _____ Him not. Neither were they _____, but became vain in their _____, and their heart was _____. Professing to be _____, they became _____.

9. In verse 23-25, Paul tells us that they lived a life of idolatry. They worshiped their own desires more than they worshiped Him. What does Jesus say He gave them over to in verse 26?

10. The final point I want to show you in this opening chapter of Romans is in the last verse. *"Knowing the judgement of God, not only did they commit such things but they* _____." God, help us to heed Your Word with our whole hearts.

I find it interesting that Romans begins with the teaching on the downward spiral, another word for "reprobation." Such is a warning to us as we battle sin in our lives. No compromise is small. They all lead one way and that way is down.

This has been a long lesson. You've done well. Hang in there.

Read the proverb of the day and write in your journal.

Day Five

It has been said that if you knew the book of Romans, you would have a basic understanding of the entire Bible. That is because Paul so effectively covered many important doctrinal issues and dealt with the practical side of Christianity at the same time. The way of salvation, sovereignty, the security of the believer, with emphasis on justification by faith and then conditions for Godly living, were at the heart of his letter. As you study this valuable book, I pray that the Holy Spirit will quicken you to underline and to meditate upon these important truths so that you might know Him and be equipped to share Him with others.

Read Romans, Chapter 2 and do the following:

1. A lot of people have misquoted Romans 2. I want you to get this. God is not telling us that you should never judge sin. In Romans 2, Paul is warning them that **they judge others while committing the same sin**. Do you see that in verse 1?

2. Write out verse 11.

_____

_____

_____

_____

_____

There is going to be a judgement. God will be the judge. He will not have a standard for one person and a different standard for another. His holiness and His righteousness will be the standard. I don't know about you but this study reminds me that I should fear the wrath of a living and holy God. I don't need to be afraid to follow Him or talk to Him about my problems. I do need to realize that He is holy and that someday I will give an account for my life.

3. Write out verse 16.

_____

_____

_____

_____

_____

God has seen everything that has ever been said or done. There is nothing that has been hidden from Him and everything will be revealed on judgment day. Are you ready?

4. Was Paul saying that circumcision was an issue of the heart or of the law?

Circumcision was an outward action God assigned to Abraham to show covenant with God. Although it was a spiritual act, it was also important physically. Since the Jewish men practiced circumcision, the Jewish women were much healthier. Today, circumcision is practiced by the world for health reasons. What God is speaking to us about is circumcision of our heart. Until we cut off our fleshly ways, we can't be clean before God.

Write out your memory verses for the week.

Romans 6:1

_____

_____

_____

_____

_____

Romans 6:2

_____

_____

_____

_____

Let's pray together.

Lord Jesus,

I know that You see every area of compromise in my life. I don't understand why I continue to make these mistakes. I ask You to reveal to me the doors and entry ways into my life that are giving ground to the enemy. I pray that I would have a renewed desire to overcome every area of compromise in my life that You might be glorified. Thank You for Your mercy at work in my life today. I do love You. In Jesus name.

Read the proverb of the day and write in your journal.

Day Six

Read Romans, Chapter 3 and answer the following questions:

1. Let's look at verse 4. What do you think it means, *"Let God be true and every man a liar?"*

2. Verse 10 says there is none righteous, not even one. How many understand?

3. How many seek after God?

4. How many are going out of the way?

5. What is their mouth full of?

6. According to the words of Paul in this chapter, "who" has sinned and what verse did you find the answer in?

7. In verse 28, how are we justified?

8. Is He God of the Jews only?

9. To be justified is to be as if you never sinned. That is how Jesus sees you if you have been washed of your sins by His blood. When He justifies you, it is as if your sins have been erased. How do you see yourself?

10. How does faith affect the law? (v.31)

JUSTIFIED

Let's look at this word "justified." When Jesus saved you, He washed all your sins away. When He sees you now, it's as if you never sinned. Justification is a divine act whereby a Holy God judicially declares a believing sinner to be righteous and acceptable before Him. This is because Christ has borne the sinner's sin on the cross and has become rightousness to us.

Imagine yourself standing in a courtroom. Seated before you is a judge who has the power of life and death. The prosecuting attorney presents the case against you. Everything you have said or done wrong this past week is exposed to the whole world. What can you say? You stand guilty, condemned. The judge pronounces your final sentence. Guilty and condemned to die. But wait! Out of the audience comes a figure. This unknown figure asks to speak to the judge. *"Sir, I am willing to die in his/her place."* The judge accepts His offer and you are turned loose. You are free to leave. Free to live your life as if you never sinned. Pretty amazing, isn't it? Doesn't it make you want to do it right? Jesus is your advocate. He takes your place!

So many believers miss "justification." Now, don't get me wrong. This is not a license to sin. On the contrary, I believe that seeing the price He paid will cause you to seek to please Him even more. Justification should free you from your past and all its condemnation. His Son's blood paid your sin penalty and your Heavenly Father's desire is to see you live a forgiven life. Let me ask you, *"Have you forgiven yourself? Do you see yourself forgiven by the Lord?"*

FORGIVEN...I'VE BEEN FORGIVEN.
FROM MY SINFUL PAST I'M SET FREE.
FORGIVEN...MY PENALTY'S PAID.
JESUS BLOOD HAS JUSTIFIED ME!

Read the proverb of the day and write in your journal.

Day Seven

In today's study, Paul introduces the word, "imputed." Everywhere you read the word "imputed" today, I want you to write the word "credited." If you put money in my account that I had not earned, that would be the same as imputed. That money, although not previously mine, would be credited to my account. God imputes righteousness to my account based on my faith in Him.

Read Romans, Chapter 4 and answer the following questions.

1. In the chapter 4, Paul again is discussing justification. Was this justification by works or by faith?

2. What did Abraham do that caused God to count him righteous?

   Are you like Abraham in this respect?

3. Who is blessed in this chapter?

4. Notice Abraham's faith in verses 17 and 18. He acted on what he heard God say. Do you operate in that kind of faith?

5. Read through verses 20-22. What was imputed to him for righteousness?

6. Notice in verse 25 that Jesus was raised again for our justification. What is justification?

I know that justification can be a puzzling word. However, I don't want you to miss the meaning of Paul's words. To be justified is God doing for us what we could never do for ourselves. Justification pronounces me as righteous as God. It is not based on anything that I have done or ever could do. It is based on what Jesus Christ has done, is doing, and always will do.

I AM JUSTIFIED!

Read the proverb of the day and write in your journal..

The Challenge of Discipleship
Month Two - Week Four

Week Four Checklist

To keep track of how consistent you are becoming in your walk as a disciple, check off your work on this chart as you go. You will either be encouraged as you see your progress or challenged as you see your inconsistency. I am praying that you will be the *"workman that needeth not be ashamed."*

	Bible Study	**Memory**	**Proverbs**	**Prayer**
Sunday	_____	_____	_____	_____
Monday	_____	_____	_____	_____
Tuesday	_____	_____	_____	_____
Wednesday	_____	_____	_____	_____
Thursday	_____	_____	_____	_____
Friday	_____	_____	_____	_____
Saturday	_____	_____	_____	_____

∞

Prayer Requests

_____
_____
_____
_____
_____
_____

Memory Verses
Month Two - Week Four

Romans 6:6
"Knowing this that our old man is crucified with him, that the body of sin might be destroyed, that henceforth we should not serve sin."

Romans 6:7
"For He that is dead is freed from sin."

PROVERBS JOURNAL

Proverbs Chapter _____ _____

_____

Proverbs Chapter _____ _____

_____

Proverbs Chapter _____ _____

_____

Proverbs Chapter _____ _____

_____

Proverbs Chapter _____ _____

_____

Proverbs Chapter _____ _____

_____

Proverbs Chapter _____ _____

_____

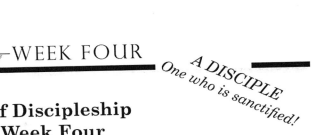

A DISCIPLE
One who is sanctified!

The Challenge of Discipleship
Month Two - Week Four

Day One

We have peace only because He paid the price. If you don't have peace, maybe there is sin in your life and you need to talk to Jesus about it. I think most of your homes have heat and running water. It would be pretty dumb if you froze to death all the time and never took a bath when those things were in ample supply, wouldn't it? Well, that's how God's forgiveness works. If you have failed in an area this week and if you are running from God instead of dealing with it, you are wasting the blood Jesus shed for you to be clean. Remember that sanctification is a process. It is the Lord setting us apart unto Himself, free from sin.

Read Romans, Chapter 5, verses 1-8, and answer the following questions:

Write out verse 1.

_____

_____

1. Why should we glory in tribulation?

2. Do you have any tribulation in your life? _____ Can you see that the end result of that tribulation is hope? Remember, the Lord Himself desires for you to live a hope-filled life. Where would I be without "hope?"

Let's pray:

Dear Lord,

This is the trial in my life right now:

_____

_____

_____

3. When did God commend His love toward us? (v 8.)

HOPE

Hope calls me to follow you Lord,
Especially when I feel I've lost my way.
Hope is the whisper of your promise,
You give me strength day by day.

Hope keeps me on my journey,
Calls me up and onward still.
Hope is Your love reaching for me,
Causing me to seek Your will.

So, we have discovered that "discipleship" is possible to us because we have been justified. Although we may make mistakes, Jesus will continue to use and change us. However, it is not a license to sin. The more grace I receive, the greater my desire to please Him. How about you? Do you realize that chapter 5's focus, justification by faith, is such an important part of your faith? It's not that we are exempt from sin, but we have the hope of overcoming sin because we have God's imputed righteousness. I know it may seem like a constant battle to identify where sin is affecting your life. As you continue in your walk with the Lord, you will overcome. If you choose the Lord every day, He will be faithful to teach you His ways as well as the ways of the enemy. Please don't grow discouraged with the battle you find yourself in. Remember, *"The kingdom of God suffereth violence and the violent take it by force."* (Matthew 11:12)

As we close out today, be reminded that our life in Christ is "much more." Every day there is more to discover. Following Jesus is the greatest adventure you can ever undertake. You may feel stuck and unable to see a wonderful future lying ahead, but God's promise to you is to always be there. Just knowing He will never leave or forsake me is exciting news!

Read the proverb of the day and write in your journal.

Day Two

Here are your memory verses for this week.

Romans 6:6 *"Knowing this, that our old man is crucified with him, that the body of sin might be destroyed, that henceforth we should not serve sin."*

Romans 6:7 *"For He that is dead is freed from sin."*

As we continue the study of discipleship, you probably have a lot of questions as to what Jesus is really going to do with your life. I hope you know that the call of God on your life will deeply affect you no matter what profession you choose. The Lord is looking for housewives, doctors, football coaches, accountants, lawyers, nurses as well as preachers and missionaries. When the disciples left everything to follow Jesus, they probably had questions also. Following Jesus is an adventure of faith—following but not always knowing where. The Bible says that Abraham went out not knowing where he was going. For today's assignment, read Romans 5: 9-21 and determine, more than ever before, that following and trusting Jesus will be the passion of your life.

FOLLOWING YOU, LORD, IS THE PASSION OF MY LIFE

1. In verse 9, what are we justified by?

2. In verse 10, how were we reconciled to God?

3. By one man's disobedience many were made sinners, but by the obedience of _____ shall many be made righteous.

4. As sin reigned unto death, even so might _____ reign through righteousness. (v. 21)

The Tension of the Unknown

All of us live with uncertainty, but most of us don't like it very much. Every day we face the perpetual questions, the unknowns of life, in the real world. What if the car breaks down on a dark road in the middle of the night? What if I get sick or hurt? Or, what if I get laid off?

We grope for answers and find more questions. We evaluate our options only to discover that we have to pick the best among a lot of good alternatives or the least bad of any number of not-so-attractive choices. We want to pick the right thing for ourselves, for our loved ones, for our relationship with God, but sometimes "the right thing" isn't nearly as clear-cut as we'd like it to be.

Some of us find security in a good job or our athletic abilities. Some of us put our trust in relationships...but what if I have to start over, or what if this marriage does not work out for me or... what if...what if...what if?

The truth is, we can never escape the tension of the unknown. We may be faithful, responsible, and intelligent. We can neither know nor control what will happen tomorrow. We can never be sure, except in hindsight, where our decisions and directions will take us in the long run.

"Follow Me," Jesus said to a lot of different people and received a lot of different responses. Some dropped what they were doing and followed Him. Some said, "Okay, Lord, but first I need to say good-bye to my family, or I need to take care of my elderly parents, or I need to pick up my last pay check, or I need to leave a forwarding address, or I need to finish this grade in college, or I need to give notice at my place of employment."

However, if we intend to follow Christ, we need to realize that we can't always wrap things up neatly, tie up loose ends or have answers to all questions. Being in relationship with God is a journey of faith. And faith, Hebrews tells us, is the *"evidence of things not seen."*

"Faith means rounding the bend into a branch of the river we have never traveled before. Faith means resting in the assurance that, although the future may be unknown to us, it is not in the least unfamiliar to the One who leads us. A future filled not with answers but with hope."

*Author Unknown

Read the proverb of the day and write in your journal.

Day Three

JESUS - YOUR DISCIPLE I WANT TO BE

In Your word I study each day,
A disciple I want to be.
Though at times I miss the mark,
I'm fighting daily to be free.

Many are called but few are chosen,
The disciple's walk to take.
I've heard Your voice whisper my name,
It's a journey I choose to make.

Following You I will find my life,
I surrender to Your will.
Grant the desires of my heart,
And my destiny fulfill.

Romans 6:1-2 were your memory verses last week. Write them out.

_____

_____

_____

_____

_____

_____

_____

_____

_____

Read Romans, Chapter 6 and answer the questions on the following page.

1. What does it mean to be dead to sin?

2. What is it we should not let rule in our lives?

3. How are we to present ourselves to God?

4. Everyday we have a choice to make. Will we serve _____ or _____?

5. Are we under law or grace?

6. What should not have dominion over you?

7. What is the result of being a slave to sin?

8. If we have been set free from sin and become a slave to God, where do we end up?

9. What are the wages of sin?

10. The gift of God is what?

Whew! That was a lot of questions and a very important chapter. I hope you got it.

Read the proverb of the day and write in your journal.

Day Four

Many believers forsake the law once they have been saved. Our world is filled with church people who practice what we call "easy-believism." They take the grace of God and pervert it. They don't keep the speed limit or wear their seat belts because they don't have to. They don't honor their parents, spouses, or other authorities. Following the Lord should produce real change in your life in all areas. In today's study, let's examine our own lives to see how we are doing in obeying God's law. Remember, it was written for our benefit. Don't see the law as bondage, see it as freedom. When we are faithful in these areas, the Lord can trust us with other areas.

The Ten Commandments

		Guilty?	Not Guilty?
1.	Thou shalt have no other gods before Me.	_____	_____
2.	Thou shalt not make unto thee any graven image.	_____	_____
3.	Thou shalt not take the name of Lord they God in vain.	_____	_____
4.	Remember the sabbath day to keep it holy.	_____	_____
5.	Honor thy father and thy mother.	_____	_____
6.	Thou shalt not kill.	_____	_____
7,	Thou shalt not commit adultery.	_____	_____
8.	Thou shalt not steal.	_____	_____
9.	Thou shalt not bear false witness against thy neighbor.	_____	_____
10.	Thou shalt not covet.	_____	_____

How did you do?

Remember Romans 3:23, *"For all have sinned and come short of the glory of God."* Because we were born with a sin nature, we have the responsibility to bring our nature into agreement with the Word of God.

Read Romans, Chapter 7 and answer the following questions:

1. How long does the law have dominion over a man?

2. Can we possibly keep the law of the Old Testament?

3. Apart from the law, sin is what?

4. Therefore, the law is holy and the commandment _____ and _____ and _____.

5. Is the law sin?

6. How do we know sin?

7. The law is powerless in itself to produce righteousness, it exposes _____ for what it really is.

8. Apart from the law, sin was dormant but the _____ aroused a desire to do that which is forbidden.

9. Are we of a carnal nature?

10. Paul serves the law of God with what?

Read the proverb of the day and write in your journal.

Day Five

Romans 8   "There is therefore now no condemnation..."

Please read Romans 8 and answer the following questions:

1. If you have received Jesus as your own personal Lord and Savior, you are free from God's judgement. Why?

2. What is the Spirit of Life?

3. God sent His Son in the likeness of _____?

4. To walk according to the Spirit is to follow the desire of who?

5. If you live according to the Spirit, where will your mind be focused?

6. Sanctification is to be set apart. To actively work toward sanctification, we must put what to death?

Sanctification. God sets you apart because you have been created for a special purpose. Because you are sanctified (set apart), you must learn how to control your thought life, emotions, and relationships. Because we belong to Jesus, we must become passionate about living our lives in a way that would glorify God.

7. "Abba" is the Aramaic word for Father. What does the Spirit of adoption mean to us who have been born again?

8. Romans 8:28 is an "absolute." That means all things work together for my good. How is that possible?

9. What is one thing you are going through right now that is not enjoyable but you know God is working out for your good?

10. Predestination means that before the foundation of the world, God chose you to be His son or daughter. Predestination is the first step toward glorification. What comes after predestination? First, you are _____ and then you are _____. (v.30)

11. Who makes intercession for you?

12. In verse 18, Paul says that we might have to go through _____ to reach what God has planned for us. Are you willing to follow Him through suffering? Just remember, God will not take you through anything that He will not bring good from.

As we close today, I want you to think about suffering in the believer's life. Can you see the purpose in suffering? If you can, it will help you understand God's ways in your life and the lives of others. Suffering exposes us to a greater need for the Lord. So, be encouraged with any level of suffering you are experiencing. Don't be fearful. You will be a better Christian for it, I promise.

Suffering will separate you from the easy-believisim doctrine of our days. Suffering can come in many forms, but it helps me to remember that God is sovereign in suffering.

Please don't see suffering as punishment for sin. Some of the greatest men and women of the faith were taught by the Lord through seasons of suffering. It's not something we need to ask for, but it is something we should expect. Trust the Lord. He is always before us, in us, and working through us to produce a vessel worthy of use for His kingdom.

Hopefully, you have studied the lives of those who went before us who were called to suffer for the cause of Christ. Corrie Ten Boom's autobiography would be a great woman to read. Jim Elliott's life story would be a great man of God to read. There are literally hundreds of others. I encourage you to read about the lives of those who willingly chose to pay the price.

Read the proverb of the day and write in your journal.

Day Six

Write out your two memory verses.

Romans 6:6

_____

_____

Romans 6:7

_____

_____

When you come to Christ, you give up the right to live life your own way. By identifying with Christ's death (remember, Jesus gave up His life on the cross so we might have life), we surrender our plans and our desires in exchange for His plans and desires. He knows what we need. By dying to our own rights, the body of sin (our flesh) is destroyed. Then we can live our lives freed from sin.

Before we continue in Romans, let's take a look at the "old man" in our lives. Read Colossians 3: 1-17. Mark "the old man" in verse 9. Before you came to Christ, you were held captive by the old man in your life. He dictated your every thought. The scary thing is that he was controlled by the enemy. When you came to Jesus and accepted Him as your Lord and Savior, that "little old man" died and was rendered inoperable in your life. Now, on any given day, you can resurrect him or your old ways right out of the coffin. Have you ever done that? I know I sure have. What do we do when that happens? Well, it is so important to go back and find out where we resurrected the old man. Then we ask the Lord to forgive us for giving something dead in us a new life. When we repent, it's as if we are nailing the lid back on the coffin of our old lives. We will have to do this over and over again the rest of our lives. If we ever choose to resurrect him, trust me, he will arise. Just as long as we walk in the Spirit of the Lord, he can remain dead. We get to choose. I want to live the rest of my life to the glory of God and not be distracted by the old man and his foolish ways. Studying the Word of God is so important because, in studying, I learn to identify those foolish ways and then forsake them.

Before we move on, I want to review Romans. Remember, I told you how important this book is for you to understand. I hope you are marking items in your Bible as you study. Today, I want to lay a foundation for salvation in Romans. Look up and write out Romans 3:23.

_____

_____

1. Who has sinned?

2. What have they fallen short of?

Have you ever known someone who seemed really good? Maybe they were involved in community work or maybe they fed the poor. Despite their good works, can you see they too were born a sinner?

3. What are wages?

4. What do we deserve because of our sin?

5. What is the gift of God?

6. What do we pay to gain this?

7. What does this scripture say about eternal life?

8. It is God's plan for us to glorify Him. However, we fall short because of our sin. What can we exchange for His gift?

9. Do you understand that salvation is free to us, but it cost God everything in His Son?

10. How final is death?

May the Lord help us to remain faithful to Him this week. May these truths be ever before us.

Read the proverb of the day and write in your journal.

Day Seven

Wow! What a week! You have worked hard and done well. I am really very proud of you! Endure until the end as a good soldier of Jesus Christ. Let's do a word review today and see what we have learned so far in Romans.

What is justification?

What is sanctification?

What is hope?

What is faith?

J UST AS IF I NEVER SINNED

E XPRESSION OF A FATHER'S LOVE

S ET APART

U NCONDITIONAL LOVE

S ACRIFICE PAID

Read proverb of the day and write in your journal.

THE MAKING OF
A WARRIOR

MONTH THREE

The Difficulty of Discipleship

Ready for your third month of "discipleship?" As we start out, I want to give you a word of encouragement. Maybe, as you have been studying "all" it means to be a disciple or a true follower of Jesus, you have become discouraged at how difficult it can be. This month, I would like to begin by looking at some of the benefits of following Him. In keeping Christ the first and foremost passion of our lives, we position ourselves for His blessings and benefits. We will study about some of those this month. So, be encouraged because obedience always equals blessing.

By now you should know that I am not preaching an *"I'll follow Him because He'll bless me"* message. The disciples, whom we have been studying, left everything. Even after His death on the cross, they still continued to follow Him. Most of them even ended up dying a martyr's death. Have you ever asked yourself what could have been the reason for that kind of commitment? Something must have called them to such a life that they would be willing to die for what they believed. The disciples were not passionately in love with His works or His power. I believe they were passionately in love with Him. Their greatest pleasure was His presence and that's what made all the difference. That is what will make the difference in your life as well. How empty my life becomes when I put myself or others before Him. I pray that you are enjoying His presence today. If you are not, cry out to Him. He desires fellowship with you—everyday.

Fellowship requires a time of being still before Him. I know from personal experience accomplishing that task can be very difficult. Even after we deal with obvious external distractions such as the phone, people, or the television, we have yet to deal with the internal distractions. Have you ever noticed that as soon as you sit down to be quiet, you think of many things you need to do? I have found that having a pad of paper and pen nearby is very helpful. As you begin to think of your tasks, jot them down. That will free those thoughts from your mind so you can spend time with the Lord.

May the Lord richly bless you as you study. Seek to know the One whom you are studying in a personal and intimate way. I am praying that you will press in to...***The Making Of A Warrior.***

Sabrina Louise Miller

The Difficulty of Discipleship
Month Three - Week One

Week One Checklist

To keep track of how consistent you are becoming in your walk as a disciple, check off your work on this chart as you go. You will either be encouraged as you see your progress or challenged as you see your inconsistency. I am praying that you will be the *"workman that needeth not be ashamed."*

	Bible Study	Memory	Proverbs	Prayer
Sunday				
Monday				
Tuesday				
Wednesday				
Thursday				
Friday				
Saturday				

Prayer Requests

_____

_____

_____

_____

_____

Memory Verses
Month Three - Week One

Romans 8:1
"There is therefore now no condemnation to them which are in Christ Jesus, who walk not after the flesh, but after the Spirit."

Romans 8:28
"And we know that all things work together for good to them that love God, to them who are the called according to his purpose."

PROVERBS JOURNAL

Proverbs Chapter _____ _____

_____

Proverbs Chapter _____ _____

_____

Proverbs Chapter _____ _____

_____

Proverbs Chapter _____ _____

_____

Proverbs Chapter _____ _____

_____

Proverbs Chapter _____ _____

_____

Proverbs Chapter _____ _____

_____

A DISCIPLE
One who puts in the effort!

The Difficulty of Discipleship
Month Three - Week One

Day One

Write out Romans 8:1.

_____

_____

_____

This week, as we continue our study of Romans 8, I want to ask you a question. Do you live with voices of condemnation? So many believers live with constant voices of condemnation. When you come to Christ and ask for His forgiveness for sin, He *does* forgive you. The enemy, however, will continue his accusations against you. It is important to understand the difference between conviction and condemnation. One voice is a voice from above and one voice is a voice from beneath.

To "convict" is to find a person guilty of an offense. To "condemn" is to express disapproval of. To pronounce "judgment" is to declare unfit for use.

The Lord convicts you of your sin so you can change. Satan condemns. Look up 1 John 1:9 and write it out.

_____

_____

_____

_____

Now, do you remember in Romans 3 where Paul declares that the Word of God is true and every man a liar? Let's see how we do in Romans 8.

Read Romans 8. On the following page are some statements from this chapter. Mark one of each that best describes how you feel. Be honest with yourself. We can never change until we become honest. Once we can see where we are, we can begin the process of change necessary to adjust to where the Lord is. I have found it can be easier to live with voices of condemnation than to take personal responsibility for the sin that is causing conviction. Conviction already requires change. Please learn from my mistakes and don't listen to those voices!

1. (v.25) We hope for what we do not yet have and wait patiently for it.

   We hope for what we do not yet have but the waiting is killing us.

   We hope for the best, but really do not think things are going to work out at all.

2. (v.1) There is now no condemnation for those who are in Christ Jesus.

   There is less condemnation for those who are in Christ Jesus.

   I feel condemned even though I think I'm supposed to be in Christ Jesus.

3. (v.15) You did not receive a spirit that makes you a slave again to fear.

   I don't think I received a spirit of fear because it's normal to be afraid of the dark.

   You do not have the Spirit's permission to ever be afraid.

4. (v.14) We are God's children.

   We are God's children but not His favorites.

   We are God's children—part of the time.

5. (v.18) God does not care about our present sufferings but only about His glory.

   Our present sufferings aren't worth comparing with the glory that will be revealed in us.

   The glory that will be revealed in us is not worth comparing with our present suffering.

6. (v.28) In all things, God works for the good of those who love Him.

   In some things, God works for the good of those who love Him.

   In all things, God works for His own good and forgets those who love Him.

7. (v.31) If God is for us, who can be against us?

   If God is for the super-spiritual people, who will be against them?

   With friends like God, who needs enemies?

Now, go back and underline which statement is truth according to the Word of God. How did you do? Did you have any voices of condemnation? Hopefully, from this day forward, you will agree with me to agree with the Lord and only listen to His voice of conviction.

Here are your memory verses for the week.

Romans 8:1 *"There is therefore now no condemnation to them which are in Christ Jesus, who walk not after the flesh, but after the Spirit."*

Romans 8:28 *"And we know that all things work together for good to them that love God, to them who are the called according to his purpose."*

Read your proverb of the day and write in your journal.

Day Two

GOD IS CALLING SOME OF YOU TO BE MOUNTAIN CHANGERS… WILL YOU RESPOND TO HIS CALL?

As you continue your study, I want you to realize that no matter how far you may feel you are missing the mark, His Word clearly teaches us that He does not condemn you. Satan is the one who condemns. Let me remind you that condemnation is only necessary for things that are to be torn down. Christ has come into our lives that we might be "built up." As for me, I am also aware how far I have to go. I am encouraged, though, by His Word and His faith in me to overcome the flesh and the devil through His Spirit. I have been asking myself this week, *"What is my motivation to follow Him when it hurts to follow where He leads?"* I have always known that to follow Him would include suffering. Maybe you are like me and wonder, at times, if it will be worth it. I mean, doesn't it seem like we go through alot of trials just to know Him better?

There is a story told of an old shepherd who could be seen outside his village walking along a desolate mountain. Every few feet the old shepherd would stop and stomp something in the ground with his staff. One day a young man went out from the village to see what the old man was up to. *"Hey, old man! What are you doing?"* asked the young man. *"I am changing my mountain,"* replied the shepherd. The young man watched as he carefully removed a seed from his coat pocket and dropped it into the barren ground. He then would tap it over with a little bit of the dirt. The young man just shook his head and walked off. Many years later this young man returned to the village to visit. He wandered out to the place where he had watched the old man. Although he had a good memory and even had a map, he could not find the mountain. For where a desolate mountain once stood, a beautiful mountain, full of pine trees, stood which had grown from the old man's seeds. The old man had changed his mountain.

That is what God is calling you to do. What is your mountain? No matter how tough and unfair it may seem at times, God is wanting to make a mountain changer out of you. Will you respond to His call?

As we think about the blessings and benefits of God, the first thing that comes to my mind is His never-ending grace at work in our lives. We fall down but He continues to pick us up. Proverbs 24:16 says, *"For a just man falleth seven times; and riseth up again: but the wicked shall fall into mischief."* Write out your first memory verse, Romans 8:1.

_____

_____

_____

Think about all the mistakes you have made just in the past few months. Yet, here the Word clearly teaches us we don't have to walk in condemnation. He has not only called us to be His disciples, but He has provided a way to accomplish that call. Notice that this promise is to those who walk not after the flesh. Look at Romans 8:14. If you are being led by His Spirit, then you have evidence of your salvation. If you are under conviction in any area, sing His praises. You are His!

WHEN JESUS CALLS YOU, HE ALWAYS GIVES YOU HIS FULL SUPPORT!

You are being led by Him and guess what? He has not given up on you. He is calling you to overcome sin. You never will, though, if you walk in condemnation. Receive His forgiveness today. Remember, repentance is simply agreeing with God. Practice Romans 8:1. When the enemy comes against you with his taunts, boldly declare over yourself, *"There is therefore, NOW, no condemnation to me because I have agreed with my Father and now I am free!"* Isn't it overwhelming that Jesus loved you so much that He died for you? He died for you knowing that you would betray Him and deny Him just as Peter did. He died knowing you would make mistakes. When you fall down, He will always be there to pick you up and remind you, *"My child, you haven't failed until you quit."* Write out Romans 8:28.

_____

_____

_____

As you looked at Romans 8:28, I hope you discovered that one of the reasons we can continue our fight to stay in position is that God is working all things out for our own good. One thing I have been doing lately is reminding Him when things don't seem to be going very well. *"God! You promised!"* So, I may not see light right now in a given situation, but He has promised to work this out for my good. He is faithful. Come on, let's be *"mountain changers."* In His light, there is light. Write out a prayer this morning asking Him to finish what He has begun in you. Tell the Lord exactly how you feel about your failures. Then ask Him to change you.

Dear Jesus,

_____

_____

_____

Read the proverb of the day and write in your journal.

Day Three

I tell you, being a person in love with Jesus is such an incredible thing. Most people are filled with themselves, they are living their lives in total selfishness. Ah, but not you, my friend. You are living for Jesus and He is richly blessing your life.

"Youth is not entirely a time of life; it is a state of mind. Nobody grows old by merely living a number of years. People grow old by deserting their ideals. You are as young as your faith, as old as your doubt; as young as your self-confidence, as old as your fear, as young as your hope, as old as your despair.

There is no security in this life, only opportunity.

Only those are fit to live who are not afraid to die.

It is fatal to enter any war without the will to win it."

*General Douglas MacArthur

Read Romans 9 and answer your questions.

1. Romans 9:2-3 in the Living Bible says, *"How I long for you to come to Christ. My heart is heavy within me and I grieve bitterly day and night because of you."* Are you longing for someone to come to Christ? List them by their initials.

2. Is your heart heavy for them? Why or why not?

3. Have you ever wept because a friend doesn't know Jesus? If not, pray that God will give you the heart and burden for your lost loved one.

4. In verse 4 of the Living Bible it says, *"God has given you so much but still you will not listen to Him."* Let's thank God for some of the things He has given us. List them.

   *Thank you, Lord, for:*_____

   _____

Let me ask, are you listening to Him? Do you walk and talk with Him throughout your day?

Read the proverb of the day and write in your journal.

Day Four

Do you know anyone who claims to belong to Jesus and yet lives a life filled with condemnation? Granted, if you find yourself trapped in sin, you should have conviction. But, once again, let's look at the difference in conviction vs. condemnation. Condemnation is always a voice from beneath. It condemns you for your mistakes without giving you hope to overcome. The voice of conviction, however, is always from above. It is a voice of hope. Conviction will direct you to the place where you got off the road of holiness and then direct you back to Jesus. Pray with me.

Dear Lord,

Thank You for convicting me of my sin. To be honest, I sometimes have a hard time talking to You about my failures. I know that is wrong. If anyone can understand me and direct me through these strongholds in my life, it's You, Lord. Please forgive me of (list your sin):

_____

_____

I ask You to cleanse me and fill me with Your Spirit. I thank You for Your Word which convicts me of my sin. I really need You, Lord, and I want You to know how much I love You.

The voice of condemnation I hear,
I turn to hear Your voice.
Agreeing with the Word will set me free,
Believing the truth must be my choice.

The truth is that it grieves You when I sin,
I strive to walk in Your way.
But, though I fall down seven times,
Condemnation is not allowed to stay.

Even in my mistakes You work,
All things together for my good.
You'll turn my battles to victory soon,
Then I'll be glad that I stood.

Read Romans 10 and answer your questions.

1. If you could have one wish for your family, what would it be?
Paul's wish for his family, the Jewish people, was that they would be saved.

2. How were they attempting to save themselves?

Do you know anyone like that?

3. Who is the end of the law?

4. What word is Paul referring to in verse 8?

5. What two things do we need to be saved in verse 9?

6. What does the heart believe unto?

7. Is there a difference between the Jew and the Greek?

8. What is the message in verses 12 and 13?

9. How does faith come?

10. How does hearing come?

Below, write out your memory verses for this week.

_____

_____

_____

Read the proverb of the day and write in your journal.

Day Five

As you study Romans, hopefully you are realizing more fully the call on your life to be sanctified, that is—set apart. Receiving Christ opens the door for your complete salvation, but it is only the first level of faith. There are many levels. Remember this, (1 Thess. 5:23), God desires to sanctify you or set you apart—body, soul and spirit. Even though you have accepted Christ, you still have strongholds to overcome. A stronghold is any area of sin in your life that you cannot overcome. You need to pray for your soul. Here's a prayer that I use to pray for my soul.

* Pray for an inclination to God and His Word. I must want to know God and read His Word and draw near to Him.

  Psalms 119:36; *"Incline my heart unto thy testimonies and not to covetousness."* (gain)

  Prayer: *Father, I pray that you would incline my heart to You and Your Word.*

* When I am inclined to the Word, I need to pray to have the eyes of my heart opened so that I can see what is really there, not just my own ideas.

  Psalms 119.18; *"Open thou mine eyes, that I may behold wondrous things out of the thy law."*

  Prayer: *Father, I pray that You would open the eyes of my heart that I might see things Your way and only Your way.*

* Pray that God would unite your heart.

  Psalms 86.11; *"Teach me they way, O Lord; I will walk in thy truth: unite my heart to fear thy name."*

  Prayer: *O Father, my heart has been badly fragmented, parts of it remain darkened while other parts are enlightened. I pray that You would unite my heart.*

* Pray for the gift of repentance. The Bible teaches us that God responds to our choices. If we will, then He will. If we make a certain choice, God does one thing. If we make a different choice, God does a different thing. If you return to Him, then He will return to you. Repentance is a call to action! A call to change!

  Acts 3:19; *"Repent ye therefore, and be converted, that your sins may be blotted out, when the times of refreshing shall come from the presence of the Lord."*

  Prayer: *Father, I ask You for the gift to repent of my sins that You might come and refresh me, that I might bring glory to Your name.*

* Pray that you might hallow His name.

Matthew 6:9; *"After this manner therefore pray ye: Our Father which art in heaven, Hallowed be thy name.*

Prayer: *Lord, cause Your name to be known, feared, loved, cherished, admired, praised, and trusted because of my life and ministry.*

God's plan for you is so special. He wants to use you to display His glory. I pray that today, as you study, you will come to know and love Him even more.

Read Romans 11 and answer the following questions:

1. Have you ever felt left out of a group you were supposed to be a part of?

2. Some Jewish people were really feeling left out as Christianity began to spread. They had always felt special to God. Now, as His Word began to spread to the Gentiles (people they thought were unworthy), they began to feel rejected by God. How about you? Does it ever bother you when God begins to work in someone's life that you have given up on?

Let's learn from this passage and be thankful that God not only saved us, but His mercy is extended to "whosoever will."

3. Reading this chapter has reminded me that sometimes you feel as if you are only a remnant in your group. Do you have a Bible study in your church? Remember, the very purpose of a Bible study is that you might discover other believers in your group. How committed to your Bible study are you? Would Jesus be pleased with how you have held the standard there?

Maybe you feel like you are the only one standing for Jesus. Please remember that following Jesus can require times and seasons of feeling alone. He is with you. You are never alone.

4. Look at verses 33-36. What is Paul saying?

5. Have you come to know that God's ways are not our ways?

Read the proverb of the day and write in your journal.

Day Six

Romans 12:1-2 may be the most significant verses in the Bible. They testify of the disciples' level of commitment. I am sure that you realize, as a disciple, you have been set apart from this world and its standards.

Let me give you these verses from the New Living Translation, *"And so, dear brothers and sisters, I plead with you to give your bodies to God because of all he has done for you. Let them be a living and holy sacrifice - the kind he will find acceptable. This is truly the way to worship him. Don't copy the behaviors and customs of this world, but let God transform you into a new person by changing the way you think. Then you will know God's will for you, which is good and pleasing and perfect."*

Often, when we separate ourselves unto the Lord, we will face loneliness.

"Loneliness is God's call to us to fellowship with Him. But, too many times we feel that it is a need for companionship with the opposite sex. When we are experiencing loneliness, this indicates to us that we are allowing the longings of our souls to dominate our lives rather than enjoying the ever-present fellowship of God's spirit with our spirit. As the Lord brings us through difficult times and we begin to feel lonely, we can accept this as His signal to us that at the very same moment He is experiencing the same anguish toward us and wants us to make Him our basic delight. Isaiah 62:5"

(Oswald Chambers)

To be left alone—just the thought of it can bring mixed feelings. For some, it's emptiness. For others, it signifies a period of rest and quiet. Imagine being left alone without God, like a prisoner in solitary confinement and without hope. To be left alone with Him should bring us peace. As we come to Him, as we present our bodies to Him, we find our purpose. Jesus was our example. He too had to present His body to the Father. There were many times He went away to be alone with God. Joshua was alone when the Lord came to Him. Moses was by himself at the burning bush. Plan to get alone with God. To be alone with God cannot be overemphasized.

Read Romans 12 and answer the following questions:

1. Which do you think would be more difficult to do; die for someone or live for someone? In other words, would it be easier to make a one time, final sacrifice for someone you really love or to spend a lifetime living to please that person?

2. Paul is challenging us to live our lives as a living sacrifice. The problem with living sacrifices is that they tend to crawl off the altar. How do you think verse 2 is instructing us to live this command out?

3. If you were teaching a new believer how to live the crucified life, what would you tell them that verse 2 means?

4. What are some "patterns" of this world?

5. What are we to abhor? What are we to cleave to?

6. How are we to treat those who persecute us?

7. How should we treat those who weep?

8. How are we to live peaceably with all men?

9. How are we to treat our enemies?

10. How are we to overcome evil?

Read the proverb of the day and write in your journal.

Day Seven

Wow! Did you ever imagine following Jesus on the road of "discipleship" could have so many twists and turns? That is why it is so important we stay glued to the Word of God. The Word will be our source of strength and will guide us to a place of peace and rest. Remember, following Jesus is not all battle and wounds. There are also times of refreshing that come when we are walking with a heart bent towards His will.

What we are learning about is agreeing with God. When He shows you something as you are reading or praying, just simply agree and leave the rest to Him. He is your deliverer.

I am so proud of you and how you are becoming disciplined to the Word. However, I am praying that soon you will be drawn to the Word and it will become the joy of your life. Keep up the good work.

"When we obey Him, every path He guides us on is fragrant with His loving kindness and His truth."

Psalms 25:10 TLB

1. What is one blessing or benefit you have received from the Lord this week?

Write out a short prayer asking the Lord to open your eyes to His blessings and benefits in your life.

Dear Jesus,

_____

_____

_____

_____

_____

_____

Read the proverb of the day and write in your journal.

The Difficulty of Discipleship
Month Three - Week Two

Week Two Checklist

To keep track of how consistent you are becoming in your walk as a disciple, check off your work on this chart as you go. You will either be encouraged as you see your progress or challenged as you see your inconsistency. I am praying that you will be the *"workman that needeth not be ashamed."*

	Bible Study	Memory	Proverbs	Prayer
Sunday	_____	_____	_____	_____
Monday	_____	_____	_____	_____
Tuesday	_____	_____	_____	_____
Wednesday	_____	_____	_____	_____
Thursday	_____	_____	_____	_____
Friday	_____	_____	_____	_____
Saturday	_____	_____	_____	_____

Prayer Requests

_____

_____

_____

_____

_____

_____

Memory Verses
Month Three - Week Two

Romans 12:1
*"I beseech you therefore, brethren, by the mercies of God,
that ye present your bodies a living sacrifice, holy,
acceptable unto God, which is your reasonable service."*

Romans 12:2
*"And be not conformed to this world: but be ye transformed
by the renewing of your mind, that ye may prove what is
that good, and acceptable, and perfect, will of God."*

PROVERBS JOURNAL

Proverbs Chapter _____ _____

_____

Proverbs Chapter _____ _____

_____

Proverbs Chapter _____ _____

_____

Proverbs Chapter _____ _____

_____

Proverbs Chapter _____ _____

_____

Proverbs Chapter _____ _____

_____

Proverbs Chapter _____ _____

_____

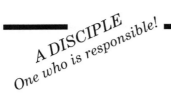

A DISCIPLE
One who is responsible!

The Difficulty of Discipleship
Month Three - Week Two

Day One

Here are your memory verses for the week.

Romans 12:1 *"I beseech you therefore, brethren, by the mercies of God, that ye present your bodies a living sacrifice, holy, acceptable unto God, which is your reasonable service."*

Romans 12:2 *"And be not conformed to this world: but be ye transformed by the renewing of your mind, that ye may prove what is that good, and acceptable, and perfect, will of God."*

Now, rewrite these verses in your own words.

Romans 12:1

_____

_____

_____

_____

Romans 12:2

_____

_____

_____

_____

As we continue to meditate on Romans 12:1-2, I want to remind you that the power to overcome sin is found in knowing and living out the Word of God. Nowhere is there more credibility to that truth than in the 119th Psalm. As you read today, apply the truth of the Psalmist to your everyday life and I promise victory will come.

"...perfecting holiness in the fear of God." (2 Corinthians 7:1b) There is something wondrous and mysterious about our inability. It is through my inability that I have found the kind of love that could produce the change necessary for me to "become one that is able." When Jesus shines His light on an area of my life where I am not perfecting holiness, no matter how small the issue, typically my first response will be my own human sorrow. *"I can't believe I didn't see that."* Followed by, *"I don't want to give that up."*

Now, I am convinced that while I sleep, there is a particular demonic assignment against the glory of God in Sabrina Miller's life which meets just outside my window. Psalms 71:10, *"For mine enemies speak against me; and they that laywait for my soul take counsel together."* As they discuss the success or failure of my day, they meticulously lay a plan to trap me tomorrow. They don't need any new tricks (not that they have any), the old ones continue to work. Hit me where I have the greatest need and keep hitting me there, long enough and hard enough, and I will begin to justify the means to fulfill that need. Then, after I've taken the bait and failed, hide it from me by bragging on me and keeping me focused on my success. Pretty nifty plan, huh? It's been serving them well since their creation. However, I'm so thankful God's plan covers even my mistakes. (*All things work together for good*...Romans 8:28)

Lord, tie my heart upon the altar
From your fire don't let me flee.
I present my body to Your will
And to Your sovereign plan agree.

To live for You daily
Is my desire it's true.
Hold me fast to Your Word
That I'll be changed when you are through.

Transform me as I renew my mind
No longer conformed to my own plan.
Trusting daily in your loving care,
Changing me as only You can.

Today, I would like you to read Psalms 119:1-24. Mark every reference to the word, precept, statutes, degrees, commands, ways and law. Pay careful attention to each sentence.

Read the proverb of the day and write in your journal.

Day Two

Authorities are all appointed by God. However, sometimes we get treated unfairly by these authorities. Maybe you've had a parent, spouse, or an older sibling who have hurt you. God sees it all and it is His desire that you trust Him with all your authorities. Many times the Lord allows your authority to make a decision you don't agree with just to test your willingness to submit. Maybe you believe the Lord has a great task for you to accomplish. Maybe you believe someday you'll be a great leader. Well, all great leaders were first great followers. Allow the Lord to use all the authorities He has placed in your life to teach you. I pray that you'll see them, whoever they are, as the voice of God in your life. Let's see what Paul has to say about authorities.

Read Romans 13 and answer the following questions.

1. Have you ever had someone in authority you just couldn't get along with?

2. According to verse 1, who ordains these authorities?

3. Have you ever realized that you are rebelling against God when you rebel against your God-ordained authorities?

4. If you can't change the situation and have an authority you feel is treating you unfairly, what is the best way to handle the situation?

5. In verse 8, what is Paul telling us we owe to each other?

6. According to verses 11 and 12, what time is it?

7. Because of that, how should we live? (v. 13)

8. According to verse 14, how can we accomplish that?

We are at war with the flesh everyday. We wonder if this battle will ever be won! May I encourage you to celebrate small victories. There is so much to be learned in the process of failure.

1. When I fail today, God is preparing me to succeed tomorrow.

   * His exposure of my weakness produces a new level of vulnerability to depend upon Him alone for my strength.

   * My newly received grace and mercy from His heart increases my desire to do it right simply because I love Him so.

2. When I fail in insignificant things, He is preparing me to succeed in the important.

   * God tests me where I can fail and few know, that He might break me in an area. (He protects His name, not mine.)

   * He is preparing me to be trustworthy of bearing His name in the important matters of the Kingdom.

It seems to me I have been learning a lot more from my mistakes than my successes lately. That has gotten me wondering exactly what God is up to. Because we have already settled that everything is spiritual, could my mistakes be being used for my good? I know that only God can place in my heart the direction I need to accomplish His kingdom purpose for my life. His anger would destroy me but His judgement brings the necessary adjustments in my life. The battle against the flesh may continue, but remember to celebrate small victories.

Write down one area you have been battling recently and ask the Lord to give you the victory there. Today, recommit yourself to take a stand in that area and determine to live with an expectation of victory.

Read the proverb of the day and write in your journal.

Day Three

In 1989, I was sick and bedridden. I felt terrible as I had to have everything done for me. I hated being so weak and helpless. Now, obviously, I was fighting pride and self-sufficiency. Oh, how we all hate to appear weak. However, I learned some valuable lessons about the Lord during that season of my life. The Lord makes us strong in many areas because He wants to use us, but we must learn to surrender that strength to Him. If we don't, we'll be proud and our attitude toward others who may be in a weak season of their lives will be wrong. Remember, we are seeking Christ-likeness in every area of our lives. Paul is teaching us our responsibilities toward the weak in this chapter. The Lord wants us to consider our weaker brother and make adjustments according to their needs.

If we are going to live in the Spirit, we need to be aware of the Spirit, right? I do not believe I would have had the awareness of the Spirit in my own life as I do today separate from the pain I have experienced. Pain, loss, sorrow—some physical, some emotional, some pain from others, and some self-induced through my own personal sin. Physical and emotional pain has driven me deep within myself to discover the kingdom of God identified in our Christian terminology as "my spirit." It runs deep. So deep it can't be fully contained within me. It constantly seeks an outlet...worship, study, writing poetry, sharing a word with a willing, or not so willing, trapped listener. My spirit craves heaven where it will no longer need an outlet, but will be free to express eternally it's desire to know and be known by it's creator. Those who can't clearly identify their spirit have one of the two following predicaments in their life: 1) They've never suffered enough to be driven to know, and 2) they are simply religious, soul driven-people who are living absent from the kingdom of God!

You may be asking, is it possible to inherit the kingdom of God and not live in it now? I do believe so. You can come to the cross and receive forgiveness but not be appropriating it in your daily life. There is no Spirit-filled living on a daily basis without the cross. The cross exposes our inability to suffer, to trust, to wait, even to carry hope! Through darkness, denial of your own personal dreams, rejection of family and friends, the cross separates you once and for all to die daily and to live forever eternally. The Spirit-led life is the evidence of resurrection power at work. No cross, no resurrection, no resurrection, no power, no power, no Spirit. However, find a believer who's walked to the cross, died through the cross, and come alive in the cross and you will find the kind of believer we want to be. I crave heaven. No limits, no boundaries. The Word will be life and that life will completely engulf every eternal moment. That is why I am so excited about knowing it, getting it so deep in me that it can bring life like that to me today. Heaven on earth. Not all days does my Spirit lead, however. I can do everything right and awaken to a soulish day, a day where my mind, will, and emotions refuse the cross. I am the only one who can overcome the loss of headship in my body! Will the Spirit lead or the soul man?

Until I decide, I am not fit to be a mother, a wife, or a friend. Sin opposes the life I speak of by painting pictures, dreaming dreams that feed desire contrary to this Spirit-fed and Spirit-led life. It perverts the gifts of the Spirit by deceiving me into adoring and seeking the gifts of my beloved more than Him! Let's face it, this life is beyond our reach, just outside our natural grasp. It takes a supernatural act of God to cause a believer to desire Him above all else. I believe another word for that is revival.

Revival is not for the doubting unbeliever, their greatest need is for salvation. Revival is for the weary, the believer who has lost his joy, his passion. Passion that is not being freely expressed is love that will become stagnant and bitter. It is passion on the death march to "practicing" Christianity, "performing" Christianity, even "perfecting" Christianity, which is a subtle form of witchcraft. (*"Jesus I know, and Paul I know; but who are ye?"* Acts 19:15b) We need sovereign grace to do for us what we could never do for ourselves, and that is desire Christ in His passion. Full circle back to the cross and into the passion that purifies love at all costs! Christianity, in it's purest form, is total delight and total desire in the relationship alone. Not church, not works, just simple love. When revival comes to you, heaven will be so close you'll wonder where life ends and heaven begins or where heaven begins and life ends. Psalms 27:13, *"I had fainted, unless I had believed to see the goodness of the Lord in the land of the living."*

Read Romans 14 and answer the following questions:

1. Has there ever been a stronger Christian help you in a particular area?

2. Who was it?

3. Sometimes we expect new believers to automatically be as strong as we are. Here Paul is instructing us to have compassion on the weaker brother. What would be one area a new believer might struggle with?

4. Who will stand at the judgment seat of Christ?

5.   Are you prepared?

6.   How many knees will bow to the Lord?

7.   How many tongues will confess to God?

8.   How many of us will give an account to God?

9.   What does the kingdom of God consist of?

10.   What things are we to follow after?

Have a blessed day!

Read the proverb of the day and write in your journal.

Day Four

Read Romans 15 and answer your questions.

1. Paul is encouraging the believers at Rome to live in unity. There may be times where God will require you, as the the stronger brother, to bear with your weaker brother. Let's look at some possible circumstances you might deal with:

   a) It may be that a friend listens to wrong music. It may be that they are a brand new Christian. Write out what you would say to them. Be sure to give them truth without putting condemnation on them. Remember, they are a weaker brother. They don't have as much light as you do...yet. The Lord convicts us to bring about change—the enemy condemns us and says there is no hope for change.

   b) It may be that you don't drink because the Lord has showed you this is what is pleasing to Him. It may be that your friend does drink. How could you best influence your friend in that particular area?

2. Let's look at verses 5 and 6. How can you tell when a church or group has a spirit of unity? What two things could you share as evidence of unity in your group?

3. What two things would you share that are evidence that you do not have a spirit of unity in your particular group?

4. If your leader didn't show up and you had to do the admonishing (v.14), would you be able to do it? _____ What would be one thing you would admonish your friends to do this week for the cause of Christ?

5. Where was Paul wanting to go next in verses 23-29?

admonish: to caution against specific faults

Unity in the body of Christ is so important to God. The Lord longs for us to get past our self-centeredness and put each other first. As you study today, ask the Lord to open your heart to see the need for unity amongst His children.

Oh God, grant us your peace.
Bring us to unity we pray.
Show us how to serve one another,
And grow in love day by day.

Forgive the hardness of our hearts,
And seeking selfish gain.
Show us that to pursue discipleship,
Only your love will sustain.

May we seek to please you, Lord,
As we serve one another in love.
May the walls of conflict be torn down,
With power and grace from above.

Maybe there is conflict in your area of the body. What are you doing to stand for unity? Walk in forgiveness and believe in prayer. May you be a standard of unity to those around you by forgiving when offended and walking in a spirit of love toward each member of the body. Be careful not to get caught up in gossip or belittling remarks about weaker brethren. May the Lord show you how to be kind but confident if you are called upon to correct others who are bringing dissension to the body of Christ.

Read the proverb of the day and write in your journal.

Day Five

Have you ever wondered why so few Christians continue to serve God when times get tough? I read recently that only one in ten people who started out serving the Lord in their youth will still be serving Him ten years later. The reason we fail is because we refuse to separate ourselves from the world. Jesus has taught us that although we must live in the world, we are not to be identified with it.

Write out your memory verses.

Romans 12:1

_____

_____

_____

Romans 12:2

_____

_____

_____

List three ways that the world has tried to conform you.

1.

2.

3.

List three ways that you are in the process of being transformed by the Lord.

1.

2.

3.

Read Romans 16 and answer the following questions:

1. In verse 1, Paul is commending Phoebe. She probably delivered this letter for Paul. She served Paul and he mentions her very highly. Is there anyone you serve like that? If so, who?

2. In this chapter, Paul expresses his gratefulness to those who have served with him. Who are the people in your life like that?

3. Who has made sacrifices for you?

4. Who has worked hard on your behalf?

5. Who has suffered for you?

6. Whom do you love?

7. Who are your good friends?

8. Who is like a mother to you?

9. In verses 17 and 18, who is Paul warning us to avoid?

10. What do you think it means to be "simple" concerning evil?

Offense always separates the body of Christ. Do you know that most people who are offended don't even realize they are? That's because the "great offender" has spent about thousands of years perfecting his personal strategy against you. When he lays a trap or snare of offense in your path, he hides it where you won't recognize the trap. It is specifically designed to attack your faith by putting you in a place where, if you don't forgive, you will begin to weaken in what you believe. For example, "Well, I don't have to completely forgive the offense. God understands and I can walk with Him and worship Him and it won't affect me."

Because we build walls around our heart when we are hurt, if we aren't familiar with His presence, we will assume He is still in fellowship with us. In reality, the walls built to keep others out actually keep Him out first of all. The most serious part of the deception is that we deceive ourselves. *"An offended person deceives themselves."* Proverbs 18:14 says, *"The spirit of a man will sustain his infirmity; but a wounded spirit who can bear?"* After all, that was the enemy's plan all along.

It doesn't have to be that way. For every plan the enemy delivers to you, the Lord has an answer, to overcome! Isaiah 59:19 says, *"So shall they fear the name of the Lord from the west, and his glory from the rising of the sun. When the enemy shall come in like a flood, the Spirit of the Lord shall lift up a standard against him."* That standard comes in your life through faith. Faith to believe that it pleases the Lord for you to forgive and overcome every offense He allows in your life. The church will continue to be filled with offense, and even worsen, as the time for the Lord's return draws near. If the righteous can't forgive, then who will be able to? Matthew 24 is a very prophetic chapter concerning the signs of His return. There we are warned in verse 10, *"And then shall many be offended, and shall betray one another, and shall hate one another."* Offense from those you love, no doubt, is the most difficult of all to overcome. After all, aren't our expectations of our loved ones higher than our expectations of the world? We know the world hates us, but when one within our own family or the church wounds us, it can be very painful.

Remember, that a person who cannot forgive is a person who's forgotten what they have been forgiven for. The spirit of offense, especially in the church, will separate the religious from the righteous. The righteous forgive but the religious deceive themselves by walking in offense, betrayal, and eventually, hate. Lord, help us to forgive. And we cry out as the disciples themselves did, *"Lord, increase our faith."*

It has been said that it is impossible to forgive a man who deliberately hurts you for the sole purpose of destroying you or lowering you. If this be true, you have but one hope, to see this unfair hurt as coming, by permission from God, for the purpose of lifting your stature above that place where you formerly stood.

The Lord has allowed me to be deeply wounded many times in my life. I also am aware of how deeply I have wounded others. When I stop to think of all that He has forgiven me for, I am compelled to forgive others. It does require choosing ahead of time that you will not allow unforgiveness to have a place in your life. I am praying and believing that you too will walk with a heart to forgive. The Lord Jesus had an unoffendable heart and that is our desire!

Read the proverb of the day and write in your journal.

Day Six

As we are studying Paul's letter to the church at Rome, hopefully you are becoming aware of his heart for the people. What about you? Has the Lord given you a heart for your church, for the people in it? Before we start our next book study, I want you to write a letter to the church in your city. Be sure to include not only the problems that you see in the church but some ideas you have to solve those problems. Deliver your letter to your pastor.

Take the time you need in your greeting and closing. Remember, you will want to encourage and strengthen the body through your letter.

To The Church at _____,

_____

_____

_____

_____

_____

_____

_____

_____

_____

_____

_____

_____

_____

_____

Read the proverb of the day and write in your journal.

Day Seven

As we have studied Romans, hopefully you have really come to understand salvation. Find at least one verse that clearly state the following truths. Write down the location of the verse beside each truth.

1. We are all sinners.   Romans _____
2. We all fall short of God's glory.   Romans _____
3. Jesus died for sinners.   Romans _____
4. We are justified by faith.   Romans _____
5. Sin entered the world by one man.   Romans _____
6. Forgiveness was given by one man.   Romans _____
7. God does not want us to continue in sin.   Romans _____
8. The law reveals our sin.   Romans _____
9. God has called us to be living sacrifices.   Romans _____
10. God wants us to honor authority.   Romans _____

Great job. Keep up the good work!

Read the proverb of the day and write in your journal.

The Difficulty of Discipleship
Month Three - Week Three

Week Three Checklist

To keep track of how consistent you are becoming in your walk as a disciple, check off your work on this chart as you go. You will either be encouraged as you see your progress or challenged as you see your inconsistency. I am praying that you will be the *workman that needeth not be ashamed.*

	Bible Study	**Memory**	**Proverbs**	**Prayer**
Sunday	_____	_____	_____	_____
Monday	_____	_____	_____	_____
Tuesday	_____	_____	_____	_____
Wednesday	_____	_____	_____	_____
Thursday	_____	_____	_____	_____
Friday	_____	_____	_____	_____
Saturday	_____	_____	_____	_____

Prayer Requests

_____

_____

_____

_____

_____

Memory Verses
Month Three - Week Three

Esther 4:16b
"And if I perish, I perish."

Esther 4:14b
*"And who knoweth whether thou art come
to the kingdom for such a time as this?"*

PROVERBS JOURNAL

Proverbs Chapter _____ _____

_____

Proverbs Chapter _____ _____

_____

Proverbs Chapter _____ _____

_____

Proverbs Chapter _____ _____

_____

Proverbs Chapter _____ _____

_____

Proverbs Chapter _____ _____

_____

Proverbs Chapter _____ _____

_____

A DISCIPLE
One who is willing to serve!

The Difficulty of Discipleship
Month Three - Week Three

Day One

Here are your memory verses.

Esther 4:14b *"And who knoweth whether thou art come to the kingdom for such a time as this?"*

Esther 4:16 *"And if I perish, I perish."*

This week we will begin our study with the book of Esther. As we continue to study the lifestyle of "discipleship," Esther is a shining example of one who was willing to die for what she believed in.

Esther was a Jewish exile who lived in Persia during the reign of King Ahasuerus. She was an orphan and was raised by her cousin, Mordecai. When the king looked for a beautiful woman to replace the former queen, Esther was among the potential candidates. We will see that her beauty surpassed all the others who were chosen. Esther is best remembered for her bravery and her loyalty to her people. She risked her own life that they might be spared.

I've known since I was a child,
The story of the Cross.
But, now I've come to understand,
That my gain required Your loss.

I walk today in victory,
Because at the cross a price You paid.
I can have peace and comforting love,
When my sins at Calvary are laid.

O Cross of Calvary!
Through Your work I pray.
I might come to know your power,
As I seek to find my way.

Read Esther 1 and answer your questions.

1. Who was the king?

2. At what time does his reign take place?

3. On what day did the King send for his wife? What was going on?

4. Why did he send for her?

5. When she refused to come, what was the king's response?

6. How did Vashti's disobedience to the king affect the kingdom?

7. What was her punishment?

8. How did he notify the people of his decision?

9. The whole kingdom was affected by the queen's refusal to obey the king. Have you ever made a wrong decision that affected more than just yourself? What did you learn from that experience?

10. Is there an area of disobedience you are living in right now?

Our choices always affect others. That's why we must learn to hear and obey God.

Read the proverb of the day and write in your journal.

Day Two

Esther is a great example of submission to God-ordained authority. Do you remember Romans 13:1, that all powers that be are ordained of God? Because Esther submitted, she received great favor from God and man. Where, in your life, are you needing the favor of God? Are you positioning yourself, as Esther did, to your authorities? I believe the Lord handpicks the authorities He places in our lives. Nothing in our lives happens by accident because He foreordains our steps. It helps me to remember this principle when I am struggling with understanding what my authority is requiring of me. This is especially true if it is something I do not enjoy or want to do.

Esther had a clear conscience and she could follow her leader. What about you? Do you have a clear conscience?

The Holy Spirit plays a critical role in creating and maintaining a clear conscience. In Romans 9:1, Paul said the Holy Spirit confirmed his conscience. Once we have received Christ and the Holy Spirit resides within us, the Holy Spirit will work with our conscience. The Spirit works both to confirm a clear conscience and to convict a guilty conscience.

We all naturally prefer to ignore our sin. The one part of us that does not ignore sin is our conscience. For that reason, the Holy Spirit deals with our conscience first not with our intellect or emotions. You might think of the relationship this way, the Holy Spirit plants conviction in the soil of conscience. If ignored, the conviction will usually grow and grow.

The conscience is an indicator, not a transformer. Only the Holy Spirit can change us and clear our conscience. By itself, all the conscience can do with a guilty person is condemn. My conscience may lend an awareness of what I ought to do, but it supplies little power to do it. The believer possesses something far greater than a conscience.

The Holy Spirit, who resides in us, supplies abundant power not only to recognize the right thing, but to do it! Because our conscience can become seared over, we must never allow our conscience to dictate to us what truth is. We may even have a wrong conscience based on our upbringing.

The word "conscience" occurs 31 times in the Bible so we know that is an important part of our spiritual walk. To me, conscience can be explained as the yes/no part of my spirit which guides my decision–making on a daily basis. When my conscience tells me something is wrong, I can ignore it and eventually it goes away. To continue in that area of sin is to allow my conscience to become "seared." At that point, it stops signaling right and wrong to me. It can also be defined as a gentle inner urging to go forward or to stop. It is a witness to me, in my spirit, of what is true and what it is not true. The conscience is the voice of our spirit. To truly walk everyday in a way that is pleasing to the Lord we need a clear conscience.

Please read Esther 2 and answer the following questions:

1. What did the king's servants suggest he do in verses 1-4?

2. Where did Mordecai live?

3. How was he related to Esther?

4. When Esther was brought to the palace, into whose charge was she placed?

5. What did Esther receive because of Haggai's favor?

6. Where they aware that Esther was a Jew?

7. In verse 15, whose favor did Esther gain?

8. Why was Esther chosen as queen?

9. What did Esther tell the king in verses 21-23?

Read the proverb of the day and write in your journal.

Day Three

There may be a time in our lives where we cannot obey our authorities. If what our authority is asking of us violates the Word of God, we know we can't do it. This is a story of one of those times. Read Acts 5:29. Peter has been told by his authority that he cannot preach the gospel. He asked the question, *"Then Peter and the other apostles answered and said, We ought to obey God rather than men."* Mordecai would not bow his knee to Haman. He was willing to die rather than deny God. Have you ever faced a situation where you had to choose between God and man? You may have to make that choice at some point in your life. Will you be ready?

Read Esther 3 and answer the following questions:

1. Who promoted Haman the Agagite?

2. What had the king commanded concerning Haman?

3. Why wouldn't Mordecai bow his knee to Haman?

4. What was Haman's response to this?

5. What order did Haman suggest to the king in response to Mordecai's lack of reverence?

6. How much would be paid to the hands of those that have charge of the business?

7. What did the King give to Haman?

8. In verse 11, what does the king say to Haman?

9. What decree went forth in verses 12-14?

10. How did the city respond?

11. How about you? Do you have the same call Esther did to serve Jesus, whatever the cost?

THE "IF" OF DISCIPLESHIP

Woe unto me if I preach not the gospel! (1 Cor. 9:16)

Beware of stopping your ears to the call of God. Everyone who is saved is called to testify to the fact; but that is not the call to preach. It is merely an illustration in preaching. Paul is referring to the pangs produced in him by the constraint to preach the gospel. Never apply what Paul says in this connection to souls coming in contact with God for salvation. There is nothing easier than getting saved because it is God's sovereign work. Come unto me and I will save you. Our Lord never lays down the conditions of discipleship as the conditions of salvation. We are condemned to salvation through the Cross of Jesus Christ. Discipleship has an option with it - "If any man." Paul's words have to do with being made a servant of Jesus Christ, and our permission is never asked as to what we will do or where we will go. God makes us broken bread and poured-out wine to please Himself. To be "separated unto the gospel" means to hear the call of God; and when a man begins to overhear that call, then begins agony that is worthy of that name. Every ambition is nipped in the bud, every desire of life quenched, every outlook completely extinguished and blotted out, saving one thing only - "separated unto the gospel." Woe be to the soul who tries to put his foot in any other direction when once that call has come to him. This college exists for you, and you, to see whether God has a man or woman here who cares about proclaiming His Gospel; to see whether God grips you. And beware of competitors when God does grip you.

* (Oswald Chambers - February 2nd)

Read the proverb of the day and write in your journal.

Day Four

Have you ever been called on by God to fast? Probably not, unless you were in a situation where you were desperate to get ahold of God. Fasting can be very difficult for you unless you have heard God and then it can be easy. You know that for a set period of time the Lord will be your strength instead of food. Fasting takes on a new light in view of your need. Esther was serious about getting God's attention. She knew without His favor she would die. Have you ever been that serious about getting God's attention?

When we fast, we need to first prepare ourselves. I do that by going over my sin list before the Lord. It is also helpful to go over the list after the fast is over! Fasting doesn't change the heart of God, it changes us and, therefore, changes our view of our circumstances.

All sin can be categorized in three areas: The lust of the flesh, the lust of the eyes, and the pride of life. These are the three ways Satan tempted Eve and it's been working ever since. It states in 1 John 2:16, *"For all that is in the world, the lust of the flesh, and the lust of the eyes, and the pride of life, is not of the Father, but is of the world."*

In Psalms 83, you find that there are ten confederate enemies of the church. I believe they represent these ten common enemies of today.

Rebellion - An unwillingness to submit to the plans of God.
Pride - A heart that sets itself above God.
Perversion - Twisting the plans and desires of God.
Lust - An inability to wait upon the Lord for our needs.
Rejection - Believing we are unworthy of God.
Resentment - An unwillingness to accept disappointment as appointed by God.
Unbelief - A heart that sets itself against the faith life.
Unforgiveness - An inability to see offense as God sees it.
Apathy - Just don't care.
Complacency - Just don't care and don't do anything about it.

Listed below are a few manifestations of these.

Sins of the eyes: Lust of the eyes, pornography, bad movies, coveting, idolatry.
Sins of the ears: Listening to ungodly music, listening to gossip.
Sins of the mouth: Cursing, swearing, lying, gossiping, abusive speech, dirty jokes.
Sexual sins: Adultery, fornication, perverted sex, rape, sexual lust, molester, homosexual.
Sins of the appetite: Alcohol, drugs, gluttony.
General sins: Rebellion, selfishness, self centered, critical spirit, anger, ungodly hatred, unbelief, theft, jealousy, worry, cheating, ungodly employer, ungodly employee, disobedience, bitterness, envy, greed, malice, slander, rejection of authority, bully-

ing, failure to be a witness for Christ, law breaker, don't tithe, abuse of prescription drugs.

Are you agreeing with any of the above? 1 John 1:9 says, *"If we confess our sins, he is faithful, and just to forgive us our sins, and to cleanse us from all unrighteousness."*

Read Esther 4 and answer the following questions:

1. What did Mordecai do when he heard the report?

2. How were the Jews reacting to the decree?

3. How would you react if you just heard all the Christians in your town were to be killed?

4. What did Mordecai ask Esther to do?

5. What was the risk involved for her?

6. What important question did Mordecai ask Esther?

7. What did Esther ask the people to do in her behalf?

8. What was her response to going into the king?

9. If you knew fasting would change the outcome of your present struggle, would you fast?

10. Have you ever fasted? When?

Read the proverb of the day and write in your journal.

Day Five

Notice that Esther used wisdom in how she pursued Haman. Obviously she was hearing from the Lord. Most of us would have immediately requested his death, but Esther had the mind of God. God is trying to teach us to wait on Him as He works things out for our own good. So many of our mistakes are made by making choices without having the direction of the Lord. We are a fast-food, fast-fix it culture and it takes discipline to go against the flow and wait on the Lord. Waiting on God is one of the most difficult lessons to learn. How many times have you prayed, knowing full well that you have put the matter before the Lord in faith, resting upon His Word...and then nothing happens? Before long, a rash of possible explanations or procedures tempt you:

Doubt - Maybe God hasn't heard me?

Fear - Maybe He has heard me, but doesn't want to do anything about it.

Uncertainty - Perhaps it isn't God's will.

Condemnation - It's probably because I don't deserve the answer. I've fallen often enough, God just wants me to be the answer. I'll just barge into the situation on my own and do my best.

Presumption - The key is to demonstrate faith. Believing it is so when it isn't so it can be.

We live in an instant credit, get-everything-now economy. We eat add-water-and-mix foods or drive by fast food outlets which poke our palates with immediate delicacies ranging from burgers and burritos to fried chicken and fish'n'chips. This conditions us to want what we want now on the basis of something that requires little or nothing of us. We don't grow trees in our yards. We buy them potted and several years advanced in their growth. Or, we move to another house where they are already fully grown. Waiting is not in style and patience has never been a forte of the flesh. The Word of God has a great deal to say about "waiting." Sample some of the truth.

Indeed, let no one who waits on You be ashamed....

> Let those be ashamed who deal treacherously without cause...
> Lead me in your truth and teach me,
> For You are the God of my salvation...
> On You I wait all the day...Sun. Mon.Tues.Weds.Thurs. Fri. Sat.
> Let integrity and uprightness preserve me.
> For I wait for You...
> Wait on the Lord;
> Be of good courage,

And He shall strengthen your heart;
Wait I say, on the Lord!
I will praise You forever,
Because You have done it;
And in the presence of Your saints
I will wait on Your name, for it is good.
I will wait for You, O You his strength;
For God is my defense...
My soul, wait silently for God alone,
For "My Expectation" is from Him.

If God weren't growing sons and daughters, things would not take nearly as long. Since He is more interested in our growth than He is in our getting, waiting becomes a very essential and useful means toward that end. He doesn't traffic in add-water-and-mix saints, or in freezer-to-microwave-table people. He builds with neither plastic nor paper-mache. What do you do while you are waiting?

Know that He isn't teasing you.
Be confident that He takes no delight in compelling you to wait.
He is, rather patiently overseeing your life.
He doesn't want you to drown while you're still learning to swim.
Rest, for He wants you to trust Him.
When nothing seems to be happening, something really is.
You're facing a new opportunity for learning faith, the kind that grows, not just gets.

Read Esther 5 and answer the following questions:

1. What happened on the third day of the fast?

2. What did Esther wear?

3. Did the king receive her?

4. By what sign?

5. What was Esther's request?

6. What was Haman's response to this invitation?

7. What did Haman tell his wife and friends?

8. What plan did Haman's wife and friends have for Mordecai?

9. What was Haman's response to their plans?

10. How high were the gallows to be?

Read the proverb of the day and write in your journal.

Day Six

Haman had a very selfish heart! He was so bitter toward Mordecai that the very thing he desired to happen to Mordecai instead happened to him. Remember what we learned about walking in forgiveness as a disciple? As a disciple of Jesus, we are required to walk in a spirit of forgiveness with a heart of restoration. Haman hated Mordecai and had no desire to see him restored. Is there anyone in your life you would not want to see completely restored to God and His blessings?

> **Restored:** *To give back something taken away...to bring back to a former or normal condition...to put a person back in a position or place.*

No one would choose to suffer, but God seems to allow it in His children's lives. I too would never have chosen the family I was born into or the suffering God has chosen for my life. But, I have bought into the Immanuel Baptist creed that truly ALL things can work together for my good. I would like to share some of the principles God is teaching me concerning suffering. Everyone talks about the story of Job and his suffering, but do you realize that in the final chapter of Job, we are told that Job received twice as much from the Lord as he had before the suffering stage of his life? Take heart if you find yourself in a season of suffering. God is simply preparing you for great things. In the book of Jeremiah 33:3, it says, *"Call unto me, and I will answer thee, and show thee great and mighty things, which thou knowest not."*

1. Suffering takes us past our "common sense" to "spiritual sense."

2. Suffering positions us to make choices beyond our "faith ability."

3. Suffering takes us from our "vision" to God's kingdom "vision" for our life.

4. He who has suffered has ceased from sin!

No matter the suffering you may be in right now, God is presently preparing an "expected end" for you. Endure to the end and discover the "blessings of sufferings." It is "knowing Him." A few of the personal things I have learned could be summed up this way:

In the blessing of abandonment, your loss of identity produces a great need for God.

In the blessing of abuse, you are stripped of pride and receive deeper levels of forgiveness.

In the blessing of sickness; the separation produces a new dependence on God.

In the blessing of betrayal; your pain produces a purification of your love for God.

In the blessing of failure; you receive compassion for those who fail.

Also, consider;

· Healing is not the absence of pain in your life.

· Healing is being able to abide in Christ.

· The need for comfort draws you to Christ.

He doesn't comfort us to make us comfortable, but He comforts us to make us comforters.

Read Esther 6 and answer the following questions:

1. What did the king discover on the night he couldn't sleep?

2. How was Haman tricked in this chapter?

3 What was Haman's response to carrying out the king's orders for Mordecai?

4. What was Haman's wife response when she heard what had happened? (v.13)

Lord Jesus, thank You for the lessons we are learning through suffering. We want to be quick to learn so we can finish the season of suffering. We ask You to equip us with a heart like Yours, an unoffendable heart to glorify the Father. We ask You to open our eyes to these lessons. We know that we so easily focus our eyes on ourselves when things don't go our way. Teach us to cry out to You until peace returns to our lives. I testify that You bring good out of everything that comes into our lives. Just knowing You more is enough! I love You. In Jesus name. Amen.

Read the proverb of the day and write in your journal.

Day Seven

You are encouraging me to suffer
I must be sitting in the wrong seat.
Well, yes I'm interested in blessings!
Why else would I be at this year's retreat?

Well, my friend I've news to give you
Bumps and bruises are in God's plan.
What you do with the sorrow He sends you
Be the one who stood or the one who ran?

Suffering is simply God' scalpel
Only thru pain can your heart truly change.
He alone knows the level of sorrow
Can you trust Him your heart to rearrange?

If you're suffering remember you have been chosen
He's promised that He will bring you through.
Then He'll use you to free others
He has NO DOUBT, for suffering qualifies you.

Don't worry about asking for it
Trust me - stay in process - it'll come.
All who love Him are going to suffer
It's a destiny you can't run from.

Lord Jesus give us grace to trust You
May we choose Your kingdom way.
We have set our heart to please You
And to Your kingdom purpose stay.

Read the proverb of the day and write in your journal.

The Difficulty of Discipleship
Month Three - Week Four

Week Four Checklist

To keep track of how consistent you are becoming in your walk as a disciple, check off your work on this chart as you go. You will either be encouraged as you see your progress or challenged as you see your inconsistency. I am praying that you will be the *"workman that needeth not be ashamed."*

	Bible Study	Memory	Proverbs	Prayer
Sunday	_____	_____	_____	_____
Monday	_____	_____	_____	_____
Tuesday	_____	_____	_____	_____
Wednesday	_____	_____	_____	_____
Thursday	_____	_____	_____	_____
Friday	_____	_____	_____	_____
Saturday	_____	_____	_____	_____

Prayer Requests

_____

_____

_____

_____

_____

Memory Verses
Month Three - Week Four

Joshua 1:9a
"Have not I commanded thee? Be strong and of a good courage; be not afraid, neither be thou dismayed."

Joshua 1:9b
"For the Lord thy God is with thee withersoever thou goest."

PROVERBS JOURNAL

Proverbs Chapter _____ _____

_____

Proverbs Chapter _____ _____

_____

Proverbs Chapter _____ _____

_____

Proverbs Chapter _____ _____

_____

Proverbs Chapter _____ _____

_____

Proverbs Chapter _____ _____

_____

Proverbs Chapter _____ _____

_____

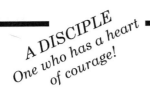

A DISCIPLE
One who has a heart
of courage!

The Difficulty of Discipleship
Month Three - Week Four

Day One

These are your memory verses.

Joshua 1:9a *"Have not I commanded thee? Be strong and of a good courage; be not afraid, neither be thou dismayed."*

Joshua 1:9b *"For the Lord thy God is with thee whithersoever thou goest."*

As we continue our study of Esther, let me remind you Esther had a heart of courage as she stood for the Lord. Courage comes from knowing you are invincible until you have completed the work God has given you to do. You may face fear at times, but you can know that the Lord is going to protect you as you follow Him. God created you with a purpose and He is responsible to see you through life. Our part is to stay rightly connected to Him. If you find yourself lacking courage in a situation, ask the Lord for courage.

Courage: *The attitude of facing and dealing with anything recognized as dangerous, difficult or painful instead of withdrawing from it; quality of being fearless or brave; valor.....*

IT HAS BEEN WRITTEN THAT THE MEASURE OF A
WARRIOR IS THE LOYALTY OF HIS FRIENDS
AND THE QUALITY OF HIS ENEMIES...

Read Esther 7 and answer the following questions:

1. What was Esther's request to the king?

2. What happened while the king was walking in the garden?

3. What did the king say to Haman upon his return?

4. What was the king's judgment toward Haman?

5. Do you think it was a fair judgment?

In Psalms 7:15, it says that our enemies will be cast into the very pit they have dug for us. That is exactly what happened to Haman. He was hung on the very gallows he had built for Mordecai. God honored Esther's faith and her courage. Would you be willing to lay down your life for your family or friends? God is calling you to do that very thing. He wants you to live your life so Jesus will be lifted up and others will be drawn to Him through your life.

Do you know someone who needs a heart of courage right now? Look back at the definition of courage and pray for that person.

Dear Lord,

_____

_____

_____

_____

_____

_____

_____

_____

_____

_____

_____

Read the proverb of the day and write in your journal.

Day Two

Read Esther 8 and answer the following questions:

1. In verse 1, what did the king give to Esther?

2. In verse 2, what did the king do for Mordecai?

3, When Esther found favor in the king's eyes, what did she ask for?

4. Was her request granted?

5, In verse 15, how did Mordecai go out? What was he wearing?

6. In verses 16 and 17, what was the response of the Jews to all this?

7. Why do you think many people became Jews?

I can't even imagine how afraid Esther must have felt. I know there are times that I have been afraid. The enemy comes and convinces me that God will not hear my request. Yet, so many times, the Lord has granted favor and I am so grateful. May I share with you that no matter what you are facing today, His scepter of righteousness is extended toward you. May you make your requests known to the King of Kings. And may you be encouraged as you see His mighty arm stretched out to deliver Esther and her people. Our world needs to see a people who trust their God and walk courageously through these troubled times. Whether we realize it or not, people are drawn to courage. Who wants to follow a leader who is fearful?

As you live your life out this week, look for opportunities to exhibit a life of courage. Please don't allow your family's history of failures or your own history of failure to limit who you can become. God takes little and He uses it for big things. Just to live trusting Him in the face of danger will impact those around you. Many will come to Him through your choice to trust Him in spite of difficult circumstances. Male or female, may we have the heart of Esther, a courageous servant's heart.

A HEART OF COURAGE

Lord, grant us a heart of courage,
Trusting in Your sovereign grace.
May we trust Your will like Esther did,
No matter the situation we might face.

Expose our selfishness, O Lord,
That we might be wholly restored.
May our love for others motivate our lives,
That we'll be more than we were before.

Fulfill our destiny, we pray,
Make the right choice very clear.
Free us, O Lord,
From our insecurities and fear.

We want to hear Your voice,
And obey no matter the cost.
Pleasing You is the passion of our lives,
We count everything else but lost.

Read the proverb of the day and write in your journal.

Day Three

Read Esther 9 and answer the following questions:

1. As the Jews began to lay siege upon their enemies, how did the enemies respond? (v.2)

2. Who helped the Jews?

3. How many men were killed in the palace?

4. What was Esther's request in verse 13?

5. Did the king follow through with her request?

6. Where was the decree given?

7. How many sons did Haman have?

8. Does your sin affect others?

9. Esther declared that a day should be set aside as a memorial to what the Lord had done in response to their fasting and prayer. What were these days called?

10. Would you say that God honored all that Esther had petitioned Him for?

Read Esther 10 and list five things concerning Mordecai:

1.

2.

3.

4.

5.

An entire country was saved because of one woman's faith. Esther believed, but more importantly, she was obedient to her uncle. Have you ever wondered how much greater the Lord could use us if we would only honor our authority? It is surely one of the greatest needs in our country today.

Esther had a servant's heart. She trusted and followed God and was willing to die, if necessary, for the cause of her people. There aren't too many Esther's around today are there?

When you think about your life, can you see any similarity to Esther? Is there any place you feel at risk? Do you ever feel like someone else is in control other than you?

Every day we go in before the King and because of the shed blood, we don't have to be afraid. As He raises His scepter of righteousness, we are heard. What an amazing picture! We never have to fear that He will deny us though.

As you think of the life of Esther and all the Lord did through her life, may you be awakened to the eternal possibilities for your life. You may think you are just one person, but one person, completely surrendered to the heart of God, can save an entire country. Are you that one person?

Read the proverb of the day and write in your journal.

Day Four

Below, write out the story of Esther in your own words. Keep it simple. Be sure to include who Esther was, what God asked her to do, and how God responded to her fasting and prayers. Do you know anyone like Esther? Briefly explain why this particular person reminds you of Esther.

_____

_____

_____

_____

_____

_____

_____

_____

_____

_____

_____

_____

_____

_____

_____

_____

_____

_____

Read the proverb of the day and write in your journal.

Day Five

We have been talking about living a sanctified or set apart life of courage. Today, I want to teach you what it means to live a spirit-empowered life. We already know that we are a three-part being, body, soul and spirit. Let's think about our lives as being a series of three circles.

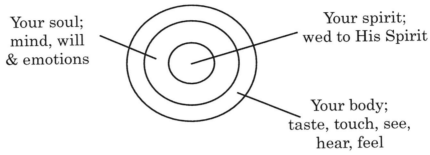

Your soul; mind, will & emotions

Your spirit; wed to His Spirit

Your body; taste, touch, see, hear, feel

The smallest circle represents your human spirit. When you receive Jesus as your own personal Lord and Savior, He weds His Spirit to your human spirit. That is the place He resides at, within your human spirit. Once this has taken place, it is impossible for you to lose His Spirit because you have now become one. The enemy cannot reach you there. So, the enemy speaks to your Soul; the Mind, Will and Emotions. This is represented in the second circle. When you received Jesus, He opened, as it were, a tunnel between the throne room of Heaven and your personal life. (You can see this in more detail on the next page.) Everyday you have to make a choice whether you will listen to the voice from above or the voice from beneath. The third circle is your physical body. Here you have your five senses: see, taste, touch, hear and feel.

Read James 3:14-18; *"But if ye have bitter envying and strife in your hearts, glory not, and lie not against the truth. This wisdom descendeth not from above but is earthly, sensual, devilish. For where envying and strife is, there is confusion and every evil work. But the wisdom that is from above is first pure, then peaceable, gentle, and easy to be intreated, full of mercy and good fruits, without partiality, and without hypocrisy. And the fruit of righteousness is sown in peace of them that make peace."* Mark this passage in your Bible!

Imagine two telephones. One from above, your Father speaking to you. One from beneath, the enemy. If you find yourself on the wrong phone - HANG UP!!!

phone from above

phone from beneath

Read the proverb of the day and write in your journal.

Day Six

In review, Satan speaks to you through your soul; that is your mind, will, or emotions. Jesus speaks to you through your spirit. When you are trying to discern who is speaking to you, ask yourself which area this thought comes from, above or beneath? Remember, the enemy wants to kill, steal and destroy. Jesus wants to edify you! Identify these areas and renew your mind with the Word of God. It's important for you to keep the channel open between you and Jesus. When you sin and the Lord shows you that sin, simply agree with Him and He will restore you to fellowship or hearing His voice. To be a disciple means we hear and obey God. Write out your memory verses for the month.

Romans 8:1_____

_____

Romans 8:28_____

_____

Romans 12:1_____

_____

Romans 12:2_____

_____

Esther 4:14a_____

_____

Esther 4:14b_____

_____

Romans 12:10 _____

_____

Romans 12:14 _____

_____

How many were you able to do from memory? 1, 2, 3, 4, 5, 6, 7 or all 8?

Read the proverb of the day and write in your journal.

Day Seven

Congratulations! You have just completed your third month of discipleship! I AM SO PROUD OF YOU! Notice the letters below. I would like you to complete each letter of the word "DISCIPLESHIP" with one thing you learned from the last three months.

D

I

S

C

I

P

L

E

S

H

I

P

Read the proverb of the day and write in your journal.

Plan Of Salvation

Salvation is God's plan to redeem fallen mankind. Today there are many widespread methods of following the Lord. The Bible, however, teaches there is only one way, through the shed blood of Calvary. It is only by going through the cross that we may obtain a personal relationship with the Lord Jesus Christ. If you have never received the Lord as your personal Savior, allow me to share what the Word of God teaches us.

1) The Word of God teaches that you are a sinner. Romans 3:23 *"For all have sinned, and come short of the glory of God."*

2) The Word of God teaches that because you are dead in sin, you live separated from God.

    Romans 6:23 *"For the wages of sin is death; but the gift of God is eternal life through Jesus Christ our Lord."*

3) The Word of God teaches that Christ died for you. Romans 5:8 *"But God commendeth his love towards us, in that while we were yet sinners, Christ died for us."*

4) The Word of God teaches that if you are willing to repent of your sin, you can be saved by faith in the Lord Jesus Christ. Acts 16:30,31 *"And brought them out, and said, Sirs, what must I do to be saved? And they said, Believe on the Lord Jesus Christ, and thou shalt be saved, and thy house."*

5) The Word of God teaches that you can know that you are saved. I John 5:10-13 *"These things have I written unto you that believe on the name of the Son of God; that ye might know that ye have eternal life, and that ye may believe on the name of the Son of God."*

6) The Word of God teaches that when you become a child of God, you are to obey Him. Acts 5:29b *"We ought to obey God rather than men."*

If, after reading through these scriptures, you can agree to the following four points:

1) Realize you are a sinner and deserve death.

2) Realize Christ died for your sins.

3) Realize that there is nothing you can do to earn salvation.

4) Realize that God is calling you to give your life to Him.

Please pray with me:

Lord Jesus, I know You love me because You died on the cross for my sin. I confess to you that I am a sinner and I see my need for a Saviour. I realize that I cannot save myself. By faith, I ask You to forgive me of my sin. I ask You to come live in my heart and be my Lord and Saviour. Thank you for saving me Lord.

If you prayed this prayer with me, please find a local church to make your decision public. Then follow up your decision with believer's baptism. I would love to hear about your decision. You can email me at www.prisonerofhope.com.

About the author.....

Sabrina Miller is a woman who has faced and overcome many disappointments in life. She has learned to give those issues over to the Lord and has found her life to be a hopeful life. Born and raised in Skiatook, Oklahoma, God has given her a passion to share His truth with others and to join Him in His work in the community.

She serves as office manager, secretary, and counselor at her home church, Immanuel Baptist Church, where she has been for twenty years. Sabrina has a leadership role in teaching through the Youth Ministry, Ladies Retreat Ministry as well as teaching the Sunday School Teachers training class.

Aside from her dedication to the church body, Sabrina has published two books. She has found much fulfillment in multiplying her life message of hope through her writing. Her writings include a poetry book entitled, *Hope Never Shouts, It Whispers* as well as a book specifically written to minister to the needs of hurting women, *A Prisoner of Hope.* It is also available in Spanish. Her work may be found and purchased online at: www.prisonerofhope.com.